"Visions, the appearances of our Lord down through the centuries, are part of His continuing ministry to us as His people. As we read the testimonies recorded in this book, we find that for the most part the Lord came to these individuals as they faced a need or crisis in their lives. These visions had the effect of encouraging, loving, comforting, guiding, affirming, correcting or teaching."

*from the introduction by Pastor Kent Nylander*

*I Saw the Lord* is a compilation of testimonies from people of the past and present visited by Christ in a time of need. Interwoven with these stories are biblical accounts of Christ's appearances and Scripture promises. This book compels us to rejoice in the truth that we worship a living Savior who is able to comfort us in ways we cannot even imagine.

---

"This book has been the single-most precious ministry tool, after the Bible, that I have ever been able to share with others. The Lord Himself drew so near to me as I savored each special testimony that there is no way to overstate the book's eternal spiritual value and blessing."

**Rodney Laymon**
**Cab driver**
**Washington, D.C.**

"With the current trend toward parapsychology, astrology and psychic power, this book is rare becauses it deals with the biblical concept of visions. In light of the outpouring of the counterfeit power of the enemy, a book that focuses on the power of the Lord is long overdue."

**Tom Slater**
**Former publishing sales representative**
**Westlake, Ohio**

"It's a blessing to know about these visions because so many people refuse to believe that there is a Man named Jesus Christ."

**Lucille Klonowski**
**Homemaker**
**Chicago, Illinois**

# I Saw the Lord

## Chester & Lucille Huyssen

√ chosen books

FLEMING H. REVELL COMPANY
TARRYTOWN, NEW YORK

Scripture texts are from the Holy Bible, New International Version, copyright © 1973, 1978, 1984 International Bible Society. Used by permission of Zondervan Bible Publishers.

Scripture texts identified KJV are from the King James Version of the Bible.

Copyright acknowledgments continued on page 204.

Portions of this book were published previously under the title *Visions of Jesus.*

Library of Congress Cataloging-in-Publication Data

I saw the lord / [compiled by] Chet and Lucille Huyssen.
    p.    cm.
Rev. ed. of: Visions of Jesus. 1977
ISBN 0-8007-9194-0
1. Jesus Christ—Apparitions and miracles (Modern)
2. Visions. I. Huyssen, Chet. II. Huyssen, Lucile.
   III. Visions of Jesus.
BT580.A1I22   1992
248.2'9—dc20
          91-35650
          CIP

A Chosen book
Copyright © 1977, 1992 by Chester Huyssen

Chosen Books Publishing Company, Ltd.
Published by
Fleming H. Revell Company
Tarrytown, New York
Printed in the United States of America

This book is lovingly dedicated
to the glory of
our Lord Jesus Christ
who so graciously gave these
visions to each one as recorded.

We also dedicate this book to
our daughter, Shirley Swearingen,
her husband, Gerald, and their children,
Gregory, Julie and Terry.

# Acknowledgments

Very special thanks to—

The Reverend Kent Nylander and Mrs. Doris Nylander for their patient support and motivation; for their willingness to give guidance and counseling; and to Kent for selecting the Bible verses at the close of each story.

Ann Batchelor, Betty Benson, Margaret Downs, Britt Boze, Alice Mortenson, Erik Nylander, Doris Nylander and Shirley Swearingen for their hours of assistance; and to Rodney Lamon and Colleen Townsend Evans for being our vital links.

Jane Campbell, editor of Chosen Books, for her patience, listening ear and ministry of encouragement.

Ann McMath for taking a compilation of documents and molding them into a viable manuscript with such loving care. All others from Chosen who have worked on the preparation of this book.

All authors and publishers who so kindly shared their experiences with the readers of this book.

# Contents

## Section 4: Yielded

## Section 5: In Times of Trouble

## Section 8: Entering the Kingdom

## Section 9: Worshiping Jesus

## Section 10: Called to Serve

## Afterword

# Introduction

The book of Acts tells us that Paul faced severe opposition to his proclamation and defense of the blessed Gospel. We read in chapter 23, verse 11, that one night the Lord *stood near* Paul and said, "Take courage! As you have testified about me in Jerusalem, so you must also testify in Rome."

And so, in a ministry of encouragement and direction, the risen Christ appeared visually to His servant, who had just been exposed to a potentially violent situation.

In chapter 24, we read that many charges were brought before the governor by those who opposed Paul. In his defense Paul boiled it down to this: "It is concerning the resurrection of the dead that I am on trial before you today" (verse 21). Over and over again as Paul went from place to place he proclaimed the resurrection of the crucified Lord Jesus Christ.

To the church at Corinth he wrote,

> For what I received I passed on to you as of first importance: that Christ died for our sins according to the Scriptures, that he was buried, that he was raised on the third day according to the Scriptures, and that he appeared to Peter, and then to the Twelve. After that, he appeared to more than five hundred of the

brothers at the same time, most of whom are still living. . . . Then he appeared to James, then to all the apostles, and last of all he appeared to me also, as to one abnormally born.

1 Corinthians 15:3–8

In his letter to the Corinthian church, Paul summarized the appearances of the risen Christ down to that day. This not only proclaimed the reality of the resurrection, but also affirmed an important part of our Lord's continuing ministry to His people.

It happened to the apostle John on the Island of Patmos; we find testimonies of His appearances in the writings of John Bunyan, F.B. Meyer, John Wesley, Charles Finney, Sundar Singh, General William Booth and many more. And we find testimonies of the Lord's appearances in the lives of many people perhaps not known beyond the borders of their own neighborhoods.

It all points to the fact that visions of Jesus not only have continued down through the centuries, but still happen today. As we read the testimonies recorded in this book, we find that for the most part the Lord Jesus came to individuals as they faced a need or crisis in their lives. These visions had the effect of encouraging, loving, comforting, guiding, affirming, correcting or teaching them.

From the tomb the beloved Mary Magdalene went to the disciples with the news "I have seen the Lord!" The Lord was risen indeed. The Scriptures had been fulfilled. We now serve a risen and living Christ.

In the Gospel of Matthew, our Lord's closing words to His followers were these: "And surely I will be with you always, to the very end of the age."

May the testimonies contained in this book be a blessing to you. May God's Word come alive in your heart and may your faith blossom.

*Kent W. Nylander*
*Pastor, Grace Lutheran Church*
*The American Association of Lutheran Churches*
*Bensenville, Illinois*

*Section 1*

# The Living Christ

# John on the Island of Patmos

The apostle John had sat at the feet of Jesus during His earthly ministry, but even the closeness they shared did not prepare John for the sight he was given of the living Christ after Jesus' ascent into heaven.

---

On the Lord's Day I was in the Spirit, and I heard behind me a loud voice like a trumpet, which said: "Write on a scroll what you see and send it to the seven churches: to Ephesus, Smyrna, Pergamum, Thyatira, Sardis, Philadelphia and Laodicea."

I turned around to see the voice that was speaking to me. And when I turned I saw seven golden lampstands, and among the lampstands was someone "like a son of man," dressed in a robe reaching down to his feet and with a golden sash around his chest. His head and hair were white like wool, as white as snow, and his eyes were like blazing fire. His feet were like bronze glowing in a furnace, and his voice was like the sound of rushing waters. In his right hand he held seven stars, and out of his mouth came a sharp double-edged sword. His face was like the sun shining in all its brilliance.

When I saw him, I fell at his feet as though dead. Then he placed his right hand on me and said: "Do not be afraid. I am the First and the Last. I am the Living One; I was dead, and behold I am alive for ever and ever! And I hold the keys of death and Hades.

"Write, therefore, what you have seen, what is now and what will take place later."                    Revelation 1:10–19

---

# His Outstretched Arms
## *Lydia Prince*

Lydia Prince was a remarkable Danish woman. A well-to-do young schoolteacher, she had been interested mostly in intellectual pursuits, new clothes and dancing. When she heard God's call, however, she obeyed and discovered more and more about the reality of God. She spent many years as a missionary in Jerusalem where she took orphans into her home. "I read the Gospel of John," she once said, "like a love letter."

---

I glanced up at the clock on the wall above the piano. It was almost four P.M.! More than three hours had passed since I started reading the Gospel of Matthew. Outside, darkness was already coming on. I switched on the light and drew the heavy brocade curtains across the window. I wanted to shut myself in with my own thoughts. I began to walk up and down the room, meditating on the words that I had been reading. *Ask . . . seek . . . knock. . . .* Certainly I had been seeking—for many months. But had I ever asked? Whom should I ask? Was Christ speaking of prayer?

In my childhood I had been trained to say the Lord's Prayer each night before I fell asleep. By the age of twelve this had become a monotonous routine. In fact, I recalled that one night I had prayed the Lord's Prayer ten times in succession, so as to be free from the burden of praying it for the next nine nights. Apart from this, I had joined in the usual congregational prayers and responses in the days when I attended church. But the thought of praying individually and directly to God—of saying words that were not in the prayer book—that was unfamiliar and frightening. Yet I could not get away from Christ's words, "Ask, and it shall be given you. . . ." If Christ required me to ask, then I could not expect to be given anything without asking.

I came to a standstill in front of the armchair in which I had been sitting. Should I kneel? For a moment I was reluctant. Then I bowed my knees to the floor and inclined my body forward over the seat, resting my elbows on the soft velour upholstery. I began mentally, *O God . . .* But somehow that did not seem right.

Was it necessary to pray aloud? The thought of listening to my own voice frightened me. "O God . . ." I said it aloud. The sound of a voice in the empty room was jarring.

I said it again. "O God . . ." Then a third time. "O God . . . I do not understand, I do not understand. Who is God, who is Jesus, who is the Holy Ghost? But if You will show me Jesus as a living reality, I will follow Him!"

And now in the familiar room, with the sound of the clock ticking in my ears, something took place for which my whole background and education had left me totally unprepared. My mind simply refused to accept what my eyes were seeing. No longer was I looking into the back of the chair. In its place a Person was standing over me. A long white garment covered the Person's feet. Slowly I raised my eyes upward. Above my head I saw two arms outstretched in the attitude of one bestowing a blessing. I raised my eyes further, and then I saw the face of the One who was standing over me. My whole body began to tremble. Involuntarily a word rose to my lips: "Jesus!" But even as I uttered it, He was gone.

Once more I found myself looking down into the chair. In the green velour seat I could see the two hollows left by my elbows. Had there really been a Person standing in front of me just one moment earlier? Or had I been the victim of some brief, incredible hallucination?

I raised my head and looked slowly around the room. Outwardly nothing had changed. Yet there was something in the room that had not been there a minute earlier. I remembered the moment when I entered the room where Father's body lay. The same presence I had felt then was all around me now. The room was actually filled with it. Not only was it round about me, it was within me—a deep, untroubled, overflowing peace.

The realization came flooding in upon me: God had actually answered my prayer! He had done exactly what I had asked. He had shown me Jesus. I had seen His garment and His outstretched hands. For one inexpressible moment I had looked into His face. I laid hold upon this one fact: *Christ was alive—eternally, gloriously, radiantly alive!* All the sum of human knowledge paled into insignificance by comparison with this single fact.

Suddenly prayer was no longer an effort. I could not hold back my words of gratitude. "Oh, thank You!" I cried. "Thank You!"

Surging billows of peace flowed over my soul. There seemed to be no way to contain it or to express it. I rose to my feet and began walking to and fro. Every few minutes I was overwhelmed with a fresh realization of what had taken place. "Thank You!" I cried again and again.

I sat down at the piano, searching for some way to give expression to my feelings. I recalled the hymn that had brought tears to my eyes on Christmas Eve. I picked out the tune on the piano. Then I began to sing the words aloud to my own accompaniment:

My Savior and my Substitute, all hail!
A crown of thorns the world to Thee assigned;
But, Lord, Thou seest that I have in mind
A crown of roses round Thy cross to bind—
Let me the needed grace and courage find!

I sang the words over and over again. Each time my voice became clearer and stronger. There was a river of peace flowing out through my lips in the words that I sang.

I lost track of time. By turns I kneeled at the chair and prayed, then sat at the piano and sang. When I next looked at the clock, it was ten P.M. Six hours had passed like so many minutes.

Eventually I undressed and got ready for bed. With the light out, I lay in bed, still repeating my words of gratitude, "O God, I thank You! I thank You!"

The next morning I resumed my reading of Matthew's Gospel at the point where I had left off the previous evening. No longer was I struggling to follow an over-shaded path through a forest. I had emerged into full, clear sunlight. I felt myself to be actually present in the scenes that unfolded before me as I read. Through them all there moved the Person of Jesus Himself—not a mere historical figure, but a living, present reality.

---

"Whoever has my commands and obeys them, he is the one who loves me. He who loves me will be loved by my Father, and I too will love him and show myself to him."

John 14:21

# Whither Thou Goest
## *Marynell Kirkwood*

Marynell Kirkwood received Christ as her Savior in what was known as the Little Gray Church with sawdust floors in River Grove, Illinois. In 1964 she and her family accepted a call to India where she taught English and journalism and Bible classes in the Himalaya Mountains. She was an effective counselor, problem solver and prayer warrior to Muslims, Hindus and nominal Christians.

---

I went to the mission field from Moline, Illinois. Going into missions, at that time, was not my choice. In our family my husband was boss and he made a one-sided decision and it didn't make any difference what the rest of us said. So finally, like Ruth, I said, "Whither thou goest, I will go—but 'a-kicking' and 'a-screaming' all the way."

I think that's the reason that when I got into missionary training at Stony Point, New York, I came down with shingles. I had a marvelous case of shingles. I don't know if you have had that or not, but to me it was the most painful, awful ordeal I ever went through. I thought all of my nerve endings were on fire; they just seemed to be flaming all over.

Finally one day I got so upset I said, "O.K., I'm not going to class."

And they said, "Well, you're not allowed to miss. We'll put the speaker on and we'll pipe the lesson into your room."

I said, "If you do, I will tear it out of the wall. I've had it." I went to bed and I spoke to God in my own inimitable way, showing all the anger that I had, and I said, "O Lord, you know how miserable I am and I'm telling you this: I am not going to be a wife. I am not going to be a mother. I am not going to be a missionary student in this school. I am just going to lie here in this bed and rot. If You want me to get out of here, You can take care of it." I don't even remember saying Amen. I don't remember anything except that I went to sleep and I slept very, very soundly.

When I woke up there were electric currents running up and down my body and when I opened my eyes, there at the foot of the bed was a figure in white. I thought, *Marynell, how did you just talk to God?* Then I said to myself, *All right, you coward. Close your eyes real tight and He's going to go away.*

After a time I felt as though it was safe and it was true, He wasn't standing at the foot of my bed anymore. I said, "I've got to get out of this bed and tell somebody." Note: Minutes before I'm going to lie there until I rot. Now, I've got to tell somebody. I got out of bed and, of course, I had to get dressed and I didn't hurt! Then I grabbed myself all over my body. I couldn't believe it! I looked at my watch . . . forty minutes had passed. I had missed one class. I said, "O.K., God, I see You are really serious about this.

It isn't my husband's decision, it is Your decision and I am supposed to go. Thank You for taking care of me. Thank You for giving me this experience."

Until that moment, you see, I never knew. Although I sang "Jesus loves me, this I know" and "He's alive, alive, my Savior is alive," I never knew He loved me. I never knew He was really alive doing the same identical things today that He did in the Bible.

That was a whole new thing for me and even though I knew Bible truths and had been teaching them for years, they hadn't gotten into the muscles of my body and changed me as an individual. From that moment on I knew God really was on my side and really loved me and would take care of me. That's when I started to walk in faith. . . .

---

"Acknowledge the God of your father, and serve him with wholehearted devotion and with a willing mind, for the Lord searches every heart and understands every motive behind the thoughts. If you seek him, he will be found by you; but if you forsake him, he will reject you forever."          1 Chronicles 28:9

# On the Battlefield
## *James Check*

James Check wrote the following about his experience in World War 1.

I remember the very hour when George Casey turned to me with a queer look in his blue eyes and asked if I had seen the Friend of the Wounded.

And then he told me all he knew. After many a hot engagement, a man in white had been seen bending over the wounded. Snipers shot at him. Shells fell all around. Nothing had power to touch him. This mysterious one, whom the French called the "Comrade in White," seemed to be everywhere at once. At Nancy, in the Argonne, at Soissons and Ypres, everywhere men were talking of him in hushed voices.

I, who was often reckless in my talk, said, "Seeing is believing."

The next day our big guns roared from sunrise to sunset, and began again in the morning. We had advanced one hundred and fifty yards when we found it was no good. Our captain called to us to take cover, and just then I was shot through both legs.

By God's mercy I fell into a hole of some sort. I suppose I fainted, for when I opened my eyes I was alone. The pain was horrible, but I didn't dare move lest the Germans should see me, for they were only fifty yards away, and I did not expect mercy. I was glad when the twilight came. There were men in my company who would run any risk in the darkness if they thought a comrade was still alive.

Night fell and soon I heard a step, not stealthy as I expected but quiet and firm, as if neither darkness nor death could check those untroubled feet. So little did I guess what was coming that even when I saw the gleam of white in the darkness I thought it was a peasant in a white smock or, perhaps, a woman in white. Suddenly, with a shiver of fear, I guessed that it was the Comrade in White. At that very moment the German rifles began to shoot.

The bullets could scarcely miss such a target, for he flung out his arms as though in entreaty. And he spoke. The words sounded familiar, but all I remember is the beginning—"If thou hadst known"—and the ending— "but now they are hid from thine eyes." And then he stooped and gathered me into his arms—me, the biggest man in the regiment—and carried me as if I were a child.

I must have fainted again, for I awoke to consciousness in a little cave by a stream, and the Comrade in White was washing my wounds and binding them up. It seems foolish to say it, for I was in terrible pain, but I was happier at that moment than ever I remember to have been in all my life before. I can't explain it, but it seemed as if I had been waiting for that all my days without knowing it. As long as that hand touched me and those eyes pitied me, I did not seem to care anymore about life or death.

I could see, as it were, a shot wound in his hand and as he prayed a drop of blood gathered and fell to the ground. I cried out. I could not help it, for that wound of his seemed to me a more awful thing than any that bitter war had shown me.

"You are wounded, too," I said, faintly. Perhaps he heard me, perhaps it was the look on my face, but he answered gently. "This is an old wound, but it has troubled me of late." And then I noticed sorrowfully that the same cruel mark was on his feet. You will wonder that I did not know sooner. I wonder myself. But it was only when I saw his feet that I knew him.

The living Christ! I had heard the chaplain say it a few weeks before. Now I knew that He had come to me—to me who had put Him out of my life in the hot fever of my youth. I was longing to speak and thank Him, but no words came. And then He arose swiftly and said: "Lie here today by the water. I will come for you tomorrow. I have work for you to do and you will do it for Me."

In a moment He was gone. And while I wait for Him my pain increases but I have His promise, He will come for me tomorrow.

———

The Lord appeared to us in the past, saying: "I have loved you with an everlasting love." Jeremiah 31:3

Even though I walk through the valley of the shadow of death, I will fear no evil, for you are with me.

Psalm 23:4

# The Revelation
## Sadhu Sundar Singh

Sundar Singh (1889–1929) is often considered the most Christlike saint of the last century. Having forsaken wealth, fame and family for Jesus' sake, he became extremely popular among Christians but was persecuted by others in his country of India. He was well received in many other countries throughout the world.

---

Even though, according to my ideas at that time, I thought I had done a good deed in burning the Gospel, my unrest of heart increased, and for two days after that I was very miserable.

On the third day, when I felt I could bear it no longer, I got up at three in the morning and, after bathing, I prayed that if there was a God at all He would reveal Himself to me and show me the way of salvation and end this unrest of my soul. I made up my mind firmly that if this prayer was not answered, I would before daylight go down to the railway and place my head on the line before an oncoming train.

I remained till about half past four, praying and waiting and expecting to see Krishna or Buddha or some other avatar of the Hindu religion. They appeared not, but a light shone in the room. I opened the door to see where it came from, but all was dark outside. I returned inside, and the light increased in intensity and took the form of a globe of light above the ground and in this light there appeared, not the form I expected, but the living Christ whom I had counted as dead.

To all eternity I shall never forget His glorious and loving face, nor the few words He spoke: *Why do you persecute Me? See, I have died on the cross for you and for the whole world.*

These words were burned into my heart as if by lightning, and I fell on the ground before Him. My heart was filled with inexpressible joy and peace, and my whole life was entirely changed.

---

While he was still speaking, a bright cloud enveloped them, and a voice from the cloud said, "This is my Son, whom I love; with him I am well pleased. Listen to him!"                    Matthew 17:5

Jesus answered, "I am the way and the truth and the life. No one comes to the Father except through me."
                                                          John 14:6

# The Great Light
## *Treena Kerr*

Treena Kerr, actress and wife of Graham Kerr, TV's "Galloping Gourmet," tells of her beautiful conversion and vision of Jesus in a small church in Maryland.

On the seventeenth of December in 1974, propelled by God's hand on my shoulder and led by my friend Ruth Turner, I found and saw sweet Jesus.

The church was, believe it or not, in a little place called Bethlehem near Preston, Maryland, and it was an all-black church. Tessa, my daughter, Michele, our secretary, and I were the only whites in that happy, lovely place. It was the first time I had been to church in eighteen years. I had never read the Bible until two days previously and I didn't believe in Jesus.

While the congregation was praying for me, a feeling of suffocation hit me with a terrible undulation in my stomach. A scream flew from me. I fell on my knees and wept; not tears, but waterfalls, flowed out of my eyes and I was saying, "Forgive me, Jesus. Forgive me, Jesus. I'm sorry, Jesus." I felt so sad and full of remorse. No one seemed to notice what had happened save my daughter; truly now, this was a deliverance, but of course I did not know it at the time.

When the congregation finally finished praying, I was baptized totally in water. Later I was asked if I would like to tarry for the Holy Spirit. I said yes, as I was there I might as well.

I asked Ruthie what I should do. She said, "Thank Jesus," so I knelt down and kept saying, "Thank You, Jesus," not understanding at all what I should do.

Finally, I was so hot and felt so ridiculous that I thought my impending commitment into a mental home was a necessity. While thinking to myself—*This is crazy! What are you doing?*—a great light fell on my face. *Huh*! I mused. *Now they have turned up the church lights to make me think I've got what I'm supposed to get!* (The suspicion of the actress mind was very much to the fore.)

So I opened my eyes and there standing in front of me was this man, all in white, with the most beautiful smile—a smile of all the love in the world, just for me. He spoke and laid His hand on my heart. To my chagrin I can't remember exactly what He said and I don't want to put words down that aren't true; however, the gist of it was, "Wait. You have received, but it's not time yet."

It was time two months later when I was in the kitchen all by myself.

I praise the beloved Lord for choosing, wanting and saving me, for like Thomas I would never have believed had I not seen Him. I was touched and completely changed.

And I pray that you, being rooted and established in love, may have power, together with all the saints, to grasp how wide and long and high and deep is the love of Christ, and to know this love that surpasses knowledge—that you may be filled to the measure of all the fullness of God.          Ephesians 3:17–19

# Jake Saw the Man!
## *The Rev. J. S. Barnett*

This remarkable story occurred sometime around the turn of the century.

I was lost in a snowstorm one night high up in the Smoky Mountains of Tennessee. Though I was frozen into unconsciousness, my horse carried me to a house. When consciousness began to dawn again, I heard a fire crackling at my feet and, looking up, saw a bearded man bending over me, swearing because I would not open my mouth to admit the neck of a bottle. In that moment of delirium, I thought l was dead and had gone to the wrong place.

When my senses returned, I recognized the man as a

notorious outlaw, a man who had vowed that physical violence would fall heavily on any preacher who dared to enter his house. I did not know what to expect.

No one could have treated me more kindly, for my rescuer and his wife did everything possible for me. When bedtime came, he put me in his own bed and never relaxed his vigilance for a moment. In the morning I was little worse for my experience, but the sun shone and the snow was melting and I was ready to go. Then it was that something said, *You have a chance no other preacher ever had. You must try to save Jake Woods.*

How should I begin? Jake was sitting before the wide fireplace as I packed my saddlebags. I walked over to him. Taking a bill from my pocket, I said, "Mr. Woods, I regret to offer you so little, when you and your good wife have done so much for me, but this is a little expression of my appreciation for what you have done. I could not repay you, even if I were rich."

"Put up your money, Doc," he said. "What we done for you was because we wanted to be clever to you. If you had come to my house last night as a preacher, I would have turned you away in the storm and been glad if you were frozen to death this morning." As I sat listening, amazed, he continued.

"Twenty-odd years ago when the Almighty took my boy, our only child, I swore that no man representing Him should ever come under my roof, and I kept my word until last night; but when your horse brought you I couldn't turn you away. Now you can go and say that you have stayed all night with Jake Woods."

His last sentence was hissed through clenched teeth. I never saw a man look so fierce. Certainly I had done all I could, and had failed, so I picked up my saddlebags from the bedside and started toward the door.

But something gripped my conscience with fingers like steel. *You must try again,* the unmistakable order came.

I walked the floor back and forth to find a ship to Tarshish, but none was in sight. I was sure that he guessed what I was suffering, but he never turned his head. Finally, I walked over to him again, and with a voice trembling from emotion, I said, "Mr. Woods, I have a little book that I want to read and talk to a Friend of mine before I go. Will you let me?"

He turned to his wife, sitting in the corner, and said, "Go ahead." I began reading that wonderful chapter in Luke, about the sheep that strayed, but was found.

There was the story of the prodigal son, too. When he came home in tatters within and without, his father was so happy that he would gladly have sacrificed everything on the place to make merry because his son had come.

Just then I looked out of the corner of my eye and Jake Woods had turned around and was looking at me with eager interest, as much as to say, "What are you talking about me for?" And, indeed, I was, for I knew he had sneered in the messenger's face who came when his own father was dying and begging his son to come home.

I dropped to my knees and took hold of God with one hand and tried to reach Jake Woods with the other, but he was too far down. I held on and reached for Woods until I remembered the subject of hospitality.

I began. "O God, I came here more dead than alive last

night, and this man and his good wife took me in and nursed me back to life, and now they refuse to accept anything for their kindness. But ever since they have had a house Jesus Christ has stood at their door with outstretched bleeding hands and with thorn-crowned brow, and they have slammed the door in His face. Help Jake Woods to tell Jesus Christ to come in today."

When I got up, Woods was sitting on the floor, looking at the doorway. I followed his gaze but saw nothing but the open door, with the sunshine and melting snow. After a minute he said, "Come in." Then turning to me, he added, "He came in," as much as to say, "You can't throw it up to me anymore."

When I left the cabin, he followed me to the gate. "Doc," he asked, "have you another of those little books like you read out of a while ago? My pap used to read about that boy, and I guess I've been him. If you'll lend me one and turn down a leaf, I might find someone to read it. I think I would like to hear it again."

I gave him the Book and he turned away, saying that his "old woman" might come to hear me preach when I returned to the Flats schoolhouse again.

I had preached at the Flats several times before, sometimes to a few good souls, but when I arrived this time the whole campus seemed to be covered with people. The first man who met me and gripped my hand until I thought I would fall off my horse was Jake Woods. "Doc, I fetched 'em," was his greeting. And he had.

I walked into the schoolhouse. The women were on one side of the aisle and on the end of the second bench from the front there was one who caught my coat sleeve as I passed. I looked down into her upturned face. It was Nancy Woods, at church for the first time in more than twenty years.

"Doc," she said, "there is something the matter with Jake."

"What like?" I asked.

"I don't know, but he ain't like he used to be since you were there. He's been really good to me. Doc, please call for mourners today; maybe Jake'll go up."

The tears came to my eyes as I walked up to the table and laid my saddlebags down.

Jake Woods had beaten that woman almost to death once because she had given a coin to a preacher. Many times he had driven her off in the storm to perish. Once, in a drunken delirium, he had thrown her into the fire. Now she had been in heaven for three whole weeks.

I turned, and there the men came with Jake Woods at their head walking as if he were on air. Just behind him was an old soldier of the Civil War, hopping on a stiff knee. He hadn't been in church since the war closed. Woods sat at the end of the front bench, and the old soldier by his side. I shall never forget how the old man dropped down and adjusted his stiff leg, then crossed his hands with eager resignation as he looked up into my face.

The house was full of good and bad. The sermon that I had prepared would not fit, so I took for my text "The Son of Man is come to seek and to save that which was lost."

I don't think I ever preached so before or since, but

Somebody standing by that table did preach that day with power and conviction.

When I was ready to let down the net, Jake Woods sprang to his feet and went down the aisle, speaking in a voice that drowned mine: "Men and women, come on! Doc's telling you the truth; for I saw that Man when Doc prayed in my house. When I opened my eyes He was standing in the door with His hands stretched out, and there were holes in them with blood running out. I saw thorns on His head, too. And I told Him to come in and He came, and I haven't been the same man since."

They came until it seemed they all would come.

Jake Woods went on to exhort and save the people of his acquaintance, and he reached more of that class in the two years that he lived than I could have reached in a lifetime.

---

I urge, then, first of all, that requests, prayers, intercession and thanksgiving be made for everyone . . . that we may live peaceful and quiet lives in all godliness and holiness. This is good, and pleases God our Savior, who wants all men to be saved and to come to a knowledge of the truth.        1 Timothy 2:1–4

*Section 2*

# Life and Death

# Stephen and the Transition

Stephen was a man full of God's grace who did great wonders among the people. A number of the "religious" men of the day tried to argue with him, but could not stand up to his wisdom, so they stirred up the people against him. Stephen's defense and proclamations about Jesus drove them into a rage.

---

When they heard this, they were furious and gnashed their teeth at him. But Stephen, full of the Holy Spirit, looked up to heaven and saw the glory of God, and Jesus standing at the right hand of God. "Look," he said, "I see heaven open and the Son of Man standing at the right hand of God."

At this they covered their ears and, yelling at the top of their voices, they all rushed at him, dragged him out of the city and began to stone him. Meanwhile, the witnesses laid their clothes at the feet of a young man named Saul.

While they were stoning him, Stephen prayed, "Lord Jesus, receive my spirit." Then he fell on his knees and cried out, "Lord, do not hold this sin against them." When he had said this, he fell asleep.

And Saul was there, giving approval to his death.

Acts 7:54–8:1

❧

# Vietnam Miracle
## *Mickey Block*

Mickey Block and Buddy Wilson were the last of the original "River Rats"—a core of forty Navy commandos trained by the CIA to run clandestine operations in Vietnam. Everyone they had trained with had been killed or sent home. And as new recruits joined them, the dying continued. . . .

To deal with the agonies and horrors we saw daily, Buddy and I had resorted to drinking, killing and frequenting houses of prostitution. These were the early days when severing ears and decapitating heads were acceptable modes of behavior, and we became known for our antisocial tendencies—even the officers gave us a wide berth.

These pastimes also helped me deal with a personal war against pain and bitterness. As a child, I'd been physically abused by my parents. Memories of that nightmare—along with the realities of my current one—made it easy for me to justify killing my enemies. In fact, I enjoyed it.

So when Dave Roever, a Christian, transferred into the River Rats and got assigned the bunk beneath mine, Buddy and I shook our heads. Only animals survived in this war. We couldn't understand how this guy could function as a River Rat and at the same time sound like a youth director from a church back home. We knew this guitar-playing, Bible-reading Preacher Man wouldn't last six months.

By this time, Buddy and I were determined not to form any new relationships because anyone we cared about got blown away. And what did we get in return? Some nut on our barge who kept telling us that he loved us and that his Lord and Savior loved us even more.

The pain from that kind of talk could only be relieved by drinking four or five more beers.

One night Buddy and I were away from the barge, on a search-and-destroy mission in a free-fire zone. That meant we could shoot at anything that moved or made a noise; we were in complete enemy territory.

It was about three A.M. Buddy and I were sitting in the middle of our patrol boat on the engine covers, sipping beer, when a shot rang out. The point man at the bow took the bullet in his chest and crumpled to the deck.

Heart in my throat, I grabbed my M-60 machine gun. "As soon as I start shooting, back this crate off the river-bank and get us out of here," I barked at Buddy.

The idea of being captured alive by the enemy scared me more than dying in some faraway jungle. What neither Buddy nor I realized was that several inexperienced, frightened American crewmen from our own barge had cut across the free-fire zone while trying to sneak off patrol early. Surprising us from the rear, they thought we were the enemy.

I opened up with my machine gun. The American crew unloaded eight of theirs right back. Literally thousands of armor-piercing bullets riddled our boat. I was knocked backward as a burning sensation tore through my body; I'd been hit. Pulse pounding in my skull, I crawled across the deck back up to the M-60 and returned fire blindly into the jungle.

Time locked into slow motion. The impact from more bullets lifted me off the deck. I could feel each caliber slug ripping into my body as I was propelled through the air. I hit the rear deck of the boat and lay sprawled across the engine pump covers piled there.

Even as I lay bleeding, the bullets kept flying. Grenades continued to explode above—and into—my body.

The engines roared and sputtered as Buddy tried to back us off the shore, but it was too late. The boat and engines were so shot up that we started to sink. Suddenly I was choking on water, exhaust fumes and blood all at the same time.

I don't know how much time passed, but when the shooting finally stopped, Buddy was screaming at the "enemy," crying and cradling me in his arms. Then I heard the sounds of a chopper in the distance, and more voices crying and telling God and me how sorry they were. I was coughing blood and starting to feel cold all over. I had seen enough people die to know I wasn't going to make it.

Suddenly out of the darkness and pain I saw Jesus hanging on the cross. Another man hung dying next to Him. I remembered from my childhood some Sunday school lesson about the thief on the cross who deserved to go to hell. Then I heard Jesus tell the thief that He loved him, and that it wasn't too late.

Because of the way I had lived my life, especially in Vietnam, I didn't think I had the same right to ask to be with Jesus in heaven. Instead, I simply asked Jesus to hear my confession before I died because I was so very, very sorry. Then everything went black.

Six weeks later, I was still hanging on in a hospital in Japan, half my left hand missing, a pin through my leg and two IV's dangling at my bedside. While looking through my chart, hospital personnel discovered that it was my birthday. They baked me a cake, sang "Happy Birthday," gave me two shots and cut off my left leg above the knee. I was 22.

During the next ten years, I underwent 37 operations to repair the damage from the nineteen .50 caliber bullets that had ripped apart my body. My psychological and emotional wounds, however, were not that easily corrected.

In spite of my vision as I lay dying in the patrol boat—and the memory of the Preacher Man's love—I didn't turn to God to help me deal with the war of pain and bitterness that raged within. Instead, I became addicted to drugs and alcohol. Even after being blessed with a wonderful wife, Shirley, and two children, adultery and substance abuse continued to lead me toward total destruction.

One afternoon I decided I couldn't handle it any longer. Tired of losing the battle against painful memories, I went to the gun cabinet and pulled down my .357 magnum. Closing the bedroom door behind me, I prepared to blow my brains out.

Suddenly I saw, in graphic detail, what would take place in two hours if I succeeded in ending my life . . . the pain and grief I would cause my family.

Broken, I cried out to God. "If You're for real . . . if You can take away the pain and give me peace . . . I need You now. Not next week, not tomorrow. Right now."

There were no skyrockets, no singing angels. Instead, a love and power I had never experienced flooded me. Once and for all I yielded my life to the One who did what years of violent searching could not.

A year later, Shirley was preparing lunch in the kitchen and listening to a religious radio broadcast called "Born Twice." Shirley had followed me in my decision to know the Lord, and the recent months had been spent growing closer to each other and to God. Now she called out and asked me if I'd be interested in hearing a disabled Vietnam veteran who was a guest on the radio program.

The subject of Vietnam was heavy on my mind those days. Several weeks before, Buddy Wilson had made a surprise visit to our home. During the many hours we spent talking about our experiences in Vietnam, Buddy told me how he had helped throw the burned body of the Preacher Man into a rescue helicopter two weeks after I'd been wounded.

That was the last straw for Buddy, who had 63 days left on his tour. He had lost me—his best drinking partner— and the Preacher Man, the only guy who had ever told him he loved him. Buddy walked into the commanding officer's quarters and announced that he was through. And if anyone tried to mess with him, he would blow up the barge and they would have to send him home.

For the next sixty days, Buddy strapped on his .45 automatic and sat in a French cafe in Tan An, drinking beer and watching the war pass him by.

Images filled my thoughts as I walked into the kitchen with Shirley. I heard a raspy voice coming over the radio. This Vietnam evangelist—Dave somebody—was talking about riverboats, special operations and losing forty percent of his flesh to a white phosphorous grenade in the Mekong Delta. My pulse quickened. Too many coincidences; it had to be. I had cheated death . . . was it possible that the Preacher Man had, too?

Palms sweating, heart racing, I waited until the program was over and quickly dialed the phone number of the radio station.

By the time the vet got on the phone, my throat was dry and my hands shaking. I didn't even introduce myself before getting straight to the question now burning in my soul: "Were you with River Division 573, the West Coast SEAL Team?" I managed to ask.

"As a matter of fact . . . yes, I was."

"Were you stationed on a barge in Tan An on the Van Co Thé?"

"Yes, that too."

"Are you the guy everyone called the Preacher Man?" There was a long pause. "I am."

"Are you the guy who slept under my bunk and kept telling me about Jesus?"

"I thought you were dead!" he exploded into joy.

"And I thought *you* were dead!"

We cried and laughed for fifteen minutes as we shared the heartaches and triumphs we had experienced since coming home from the jungles of Vietnam. Dave told me how he had cried and prayed the night I was wounded that God would spare my life. I confessed that it was his prayers, sifting up through my bunk, night after lonely night, that had impressed me with the reality of a living God.

The ultimate joy of the conversation came when Dave asked if I had come to know the Lord, and I could tell him yes!

For the next few minutes all I heard from Dave was "Praise God! Hallelujah! Thank You, Jesus! Praise God!" And I knew that our relationship of the past had somehow died and a newer supernatural one had been born. I loved the way that ol' River Rat talked!

At a glorious reunion with Dave at a church, I was miraculously touched by the Holy Spirit. A power, a force, enveloped me completely. It was so overwhelming that I felt emotional and physical healing throughout my entire being. All the heartache, disappointment and frustration stored up over a lifetime flowed out of me without my even being involved.

Seventeen years before—tormented by memories of child abuse, the realities of war and the destructive methods with which I chose to cope—I had rejected the Preacher

Man and the love he represented. Now the love he lives has changed my life and I know the Prince of Peace he serves. The war is finally over.

---

Therefore he is able to save completely those who come to God through him, because he always lives to intercede for them.                    Hebrews 7:25

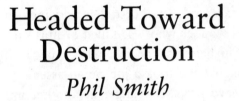

# Headed Toward Destruction
## *Phil Smith*

Only the power of God could change the life of Phil Smith, who was a violent gang leader while still a young man.

---

Why did I throw my life away? It was partly because of my home life. As far back as I can remember my father beat my mother. This caused hatred and resentment to fill my heart before I was old enough to start school. It made me hate the world. When I was nine years old my mother brought in a stranger and told me that he was my "new father."

Having no home life I found the wrong kind of friends in my Dayton (Ohio) school. As I got older the boys started looking to me for instructions. I became involved in street gangs and started drinking.

By this time the bitterness in my heart had multiplied many times. I began to form gangs in other cities and was content only when I could beat someone to a pulp. I used tire tools, chains, clubs, knucks or anything I could find. If I had no gun or brickbat I used my bare fists. I still carry scars from where I smashed car windows with my fists to get at my enemies.

There were times I would return from "lost weekends" with my face and fists burst. I would look at the dried blood and wonder who was killed or hurt on that trip.

To get in better shape for fights I began lifting 120-pound weights and took a job on an assembly line where I lifted heavy parts. My anger at another man working there had a surprising outcome.

This man mentioned Jesus to me day after day. The devil in me became mad at this. I told him never to mention that name again and threatened and cursed him. A few days later he talked about Jesus once more and I was ready. But as I started to hit him, he threw me over his head and let me land any way I happened to fall. I learned later that he was a former Judo instructor from Germany.

When he saw what he had done he picked me up and said, "Pal, I'm sorry. I shouldn't have done that. I'm a Christian. I should trust the Lord. Go ahead and do anything you want to me. I won't do anything." He stood there with his hands beside him looking into my face.

I could not help but admire a man like that who would stand up for what he thought was right. At the same time I knew I could not chicken out. Some of my gang members were working on that job and were watching. I knew that if I did not whip that man my "buddies" would whip me. They would beat me up and leave me for dead.

This is when I saw the first miracle in my life. As I started to swing, God bound my fist. I could not make the punch because I felt chained! And I could not see. God had blinded me! When my eyesight and reason returned, I found myself shaking hands with the first real Christian I had ever seen. The gang members did not kill me. God must have bound their hands, too.

I never got over that miracle. My new friend told me about some revival meetings where miracles took place and one night I slipped in. As I was watching and wondering, I saw a blanket coming down from heaven. A corner of it touched me. Slowly it all covered me. I was cleansed. I was set free from sin—from alcohol, nicotine, lust, hate, murder. Old things had passed away.

I said, "God, let me know You are real."

He spoke to me and said, *Go into the ministry.*

Just then the evangelist said, "God has just spoken to a young man in the back and given him a call."

Later I saw a vision of Christ for thirty minutes.

The Lord sent me all over America and to a number of foreign countries to tell the glad news. In every place God worked wonders. And about the time I thought I was "established" in the ministry, God spoke again: *I am sending you back out into the streets.*

He led me to set up centers in several cities and to ride among the Hell's Angels in a new motorcycle gang named "Christ's Patrol."

What a different message I have now for those who live in darkness and despair on the city streets!

---

"Come now, let us reason together," says the Lord. "Though your sins are like scarlet, they shall be as white as snow; though they are red as crimson, they shall be like wool." Isaiah 1:18

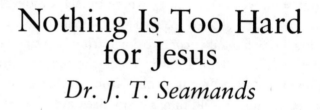

# Nothing Is Too Hard for Jesus
## Dr. J. T. Seamands

Dr. J. T. Seamands of Asbury Seminary in Wilmore, Kentucky, recounts this remarkable story.

---

A Hindu priest in India came home one evening to learn that his wife, who was in the last days of pregnancy, had suddenly taken ill and died. Four medical persons had declared her dead. According to Hindu custom, the family members had placed her body outside the house on a stone slab and covered it with a sheet.

The husband was grief-stricken and could not sleep that night. At an early hour in the morning he went out into the woods and cried out to the gods and goddesses that he worshiped, but there was no answer. So in his heart he determined that he would go back to his temple the next day and announce to the people, "Don't worship the idols any longer. They are all dead gods!"

Then he remembered suddenly the words of an Indian Christian evangelist who had come to his town and preached the Gospel several months previously. The Hindu priest had been so upset with the preaching that he man-handled the evangelist and ordered him out of town. He had threatened to kill him if he ever came back. In parting, the evangelist said to him: "There is nothing too hard for my Jesus. I will pray for you."

Remembering these words, the priest suddenly cried out in the stillness of the night, "Jesus, if You are real, then show Yourself to me!"

Immediately he saw a bright light with Jesus standing in the midst. A voice said to him, "I love you and I died for you."

The Hindu priest pinched himself in disbelief and then said, "If what I see and hear is real, then repeat what You just said to me." Again the voice spoke quietly, "I love you and I died for you."

Then the priest began to weep and confess his sins, and after some time there was suddenly a deep peace in his heart. He said softly, "Jesus, I will love and serve You the rest of my life." And then he added, "And Lord, if my wife were alive she would serve you, too, but alas, she is gone!"

By this time it was about five o'clock in the morning. His wife's body had been lying on the stone slab for almost twelve hours. He went over to the body, pulled back the sheet and lovingly stroked his wife's face and hair. Suddenly he felt her body stirring and she opened her eyes. "Husband," she said softly, "who is this Jesus?"

"Why do you ask?" he finally questioned.

Then she went on to tell him of a dream that she had that night. In her dream she was about to fall off a steep cliff, when a voice spoke to her from behind, saying, "Daughter, don't do it; I can help you." She turned to see an elderly gentleman with a very kind face. (It must be pointed out here that if the person had been a young man, according to Indian custom she would be expected to turn away from him. The all-wise, loving God was careful to reveal Himself to her in the context of her own culture.) The old man took her by the hand and led her to a safer place.

As they parted, she asked, "Sir, who are You?"

"I am Jesus."

Upon hearing these words, the husband began to tell his wife of his own encounter with the Lord during the night and what had happened to his heart and mind. He explained who Jesus is.

To the astonishment of all, the wife was very much alive and a day or two later she gave birth to a healthy and beautiful baby girl.

As a result of this experience the Hindu priest and his wife turned from their idols to the living God, and today he is pastor of a church in the Hyderabad area.

---

We know that an idol is nothing at all in the world
and that there is no God but one.

1 Corinthians 8:4

---

# The Sights of Paradise
## *Dr. Richard Eby*

When the emergency personnel arrived to rush Dr. Eby
to the hospital, they found little reason to hurry. He had
fallen from a second story balcony onto a concrete side-
walk and was lying in a pool of blood. There was no
heartbeat, his skull was exposed, his body was gray-white
and his blood had stopped flowing.

Richard Eby, D.O., physician and surgeon, who lives in
Victorville, California, tells of his amazing account of being in heaven in his book *Caught Up into Paradise.*

---

In the twinkling of an eye Jesus took me out of this
world. I cannot adequately describe the astonishment, the
amazement, the sheer shock of this event. One moment in
suburban Chicago, the next moment in suburban heaven.
One moment in the miserable humidity of a Midwest city,
the next moment in the most exquisite place "prepared for

you, that where I am ye may be also." One moment with a flesh-restricted mind, the next moment with a heaven-released mind whose speed of function was that of light!

My initial gasp ("Dick, you're dead") was as quickly followed by an overwhelming sense of peace—peace which passeth earthly understanding, peace so complete that I knew instantly it was the promised gift of the Spirit of our Lord. I had no memory about my life on earth at this time. I was enjoying a heavenly "body"; I was totally me. Aside from the complete absence of pain and the total presence of peace (neither of which I had ever known on earth), I looked like me, felt like me, reacted like me. I simply had suddenly shed the old body and was now living anew in this fantastic cloud-like body!

Being a physician, my first instinct was to inspect my new body, and I admired it instantly. It was mine all right. After sixty years in the old one it was easy to recognize myself in the new body. (I am sure that God included in this entire heavenly experience only those things that would be specifically meaningful to me, for proof and edification. He would give a different set of revelations to someone with a different background.) I was the same size, the same shape, as the person I had seen in the mirror for years. I was clothed in a translucent flowing gown, pure white, but transparent to my gaze. In amazement I could see through my body and note the gorgeously white flowers behind and beneath me. This seemed perfectly normal, yet thrillingly novel.

All this time I was instinctively aware that the Lord of lords was everywhere about this place, though I did not see

Him. The sense of timelessness made all hurry foolish, so I resumed my anatomy lesson, knowing that He would appear in His own time. It all seemed so normal in this fantastic anteroom to heaven.

My feet were easy to see. No bifocals needed. I had noted that my eyes were unlimited in range of vision; ten inches or ten miles—the focus was sharp and clear. ("We shall mount up as eagles," said King David. He was alluding to their pinpoint eyesight perhaps!) There were no bones or vessels or organs. No blood. I noted the absence of genitals. (How unneeded when in heaven there is no marriage or childbearing, His Body of believers being already completed!) The abdomen and chest were organless and transparent to my gaze, though translucent to my peripheral vision. Again my mind, which worked here in heaven with electric-like speed, answered my unspoken query: They are not needed; Jesus is the Life here. His is the needed energy. There was no air to breathe, no blood to pump, no food to digest or eliminate. This was not a carnal body of organs, mortal and temporary!

My gaze riveted upon the exquisite valley in which I found myself. Forests of symmetrical trees unlike anything on earth covered the foothills on each side. I could see each branch and leaf—not a brown spot or dead leaf in the forest. ("No death there" includes the vegetation.) Each tree, tall and graceful, was a duplicate of the others: perfect, unblemished. They resembled somewhat the tall arbor vitae cedars of North America, but I could not identify them. The valley floor was gorgeous. Stately grasses, each blade perfect and erect, were interspersed with ultra-white, four-petaled flowers on stems two feet tall, with a touch of gold at the centers. Each was totally alike! (No two earthly flowers can be identical, nor is anything else since the Genesis curse.)

Having been an amateur botanist as a schoolboy, I immediately decided to pick a bouquet. To my amazement the unexpected happened. My thought (to stoop and pick flowers) became the act. Here in Paradise I discovered that there is no time lag between thought and act. A word, spoken or thought, became fact!

(I realized instantly how the heavens and earth were so quickly made from nothing that appeared: God had simply *thought* what He wanted, and there it was.)

I found my hand containing a bouquet of identical blossoms. Their whiteness was exciting. I almost had time to ask myself "Why so white?" when the answer was already given: "On earth you saw only white light, which combined the color spectrum of the sun. Here we have the light of the SON!" My excitement was too great to describe in words. *Of course,* I thought. *He is the light of the world . . . in the new heavens no sun or moon will be needed.*

Then I sensed a strange new feel to the stems—no moisture! I felt them carefully. Delicately smooth, yet nothing like earthly stems with their cellular watery content. Before I could ask, again I had an answer: Earthly water is hydrogen and oxygen for temporary life support; here Jesus is the Living Water. In His presence nothing dies. No need for oxygen and hydrogen. I instinctively looked behind me where I had been standing on dozens of blooms. Not one was bent or bruised. Then I watched my feet as I walked a few more steps upon the grass and flowers; they stood upright inside my feet and legs! We simply passed through one another. (My Lord had passed through closed doors and a heavy stone over the tomb centuries ago with the same kind of body!)

The illumination fascinated me—not a shadow anywhere. There was no single light source as on earth. I realized that everything seemed to produce its own light. Again the answer coincided with my query: The heavens declare the glory of God; know ye not that His is the honor, and glory, and *power?* He *is* the Light of the world!

I stood overwhelmed with the sights of Paradise. God had shown me incontroversial evidence of His planning and preparing a place just for me, as He had promised. But He had more: It was music.

All this "time" (since there was no sun, there was actually no time reference) I had been aware of the most beautiful, melodious angelic background music that the ear of man can perceive. I was now ready to concentrate on it. It was truly a new song, such as St. John must have heard from Patmos. Not instrumental, not vocal, not mathematical, not earthly. It originated from no one point—neither from the sky nor the ground. Just as was true of the light, the music emerged apparently from everything and every place. It had no beat—was neither major nor minor—and had no tempo. (In eternity, how could it have "time"?) No earthly adjectives describe its angelic quality. Poets have said "music of the spheres." God has said, "A new song will I give them." I heard it—it had to be His composition—every note. Hallelujah! Music by Jesus. No wonder the cherubim and seraphim and multitudes sing around His throne!

I was not prepared for the sweetest revelation of all: the all-pervading aroma of heaven. No one on earth, minister or Bible teacher, had mentioned to me this heady perfume. Like the sight and the sounds, it was everywhere. I bent again and smelled the flowers; yes, it was there. The grasses also. The air was just the same. A perfume so exotic, so refreshing, so superior, that it was fit only for a King! Even the special formula given by Jehovah to His priests in the wilderness could not have matched this "sweet savor." Earthly ingredients would fall short of perfection. I simply stood quietly and let it bathe my being.

No answer was given my query about it in Paradise. This time Jesus waited till I was back on earth. "Search the Scriptures," the Spirit advised me. "In them you will find wisdom." From Genesis and Leviticus through the books to Revelation He has told about His love of sweet-smelling savors, His appreciation of the sacrifices of His worshipers, His demands for certain incense in Tabernacle worship and, finally, His supreme joy in the prayers of His saints. He has preserved and mixed all these together, we are told, bottled them in golden urns and readied them for opening before the Throne of His Lamb, who alone is worthy to savor their divine fragrance (Revelation 5:8).

I was allowed to share God's supreme perfume. Never can I be the same again. Just to realize that it is but one of the unsearchable joys prepared for all His joint-heirs to share in eternity is too infinite a gift to envision as ours.

And it awaits whosoever will come to Jesus! He said it; I believe it. He prepared it; I accept it.

Fortunately for me, Jesus elected not to show me more of the heavenly wonders that day. I could not have coped with another revelation. This entire experience away from earth had taken only minutes, or maybe hours. Records are incomplete. It does not matter. God's purpose in taking me there and sending me back will be accomplished through His Spirit. My mind stopped working and all was silent and black. Later I would realize that I was back on earth where the prayers of many had been answered for my return. And the next day I would hear Jesus speak to me on the hospital's fourth floor.

---

Jesus said to her, "I am the resurrection and the life. He who believes in me will live, even though he dies; and whoever lives and believes in me will never die. Do you believe this?"                    John 11:25–26

# In the Master's Presence
## *Rebecca Springer*

Rebecca Springer lived in the nineteenth century. The following compelling account of her experience in heaven is told in her book, *Within Heaven's Gates*.

A radiant glow overspread the wonderful face, which He lifted, looking directly at me. The mist rolled away from before my eyes, and I knew Him! With a low cry of joy and adoration, I threw myself at His feet, bathing them with happy tears. He stroked my bowed head gently for a moment, then, rising, lifted me to His side.

"My Savior, my King," I whispered, clinging closely to Him.

"Yes, and Elder Brother and Friend," He added, tenderly wiping away the tears stealing from beneath my closed eyelids.

"Yes, yes! The chiefest among ten thousand, and the One altogether lovely!" again I whispered.

"Ah, now you begin to meet the conditions of the new life! Like many others, the changing of faith to sight with you has engendered a little shrinking, a little fear. That is all wrong. Have you forgotten the promise 'I go to prepare a place for you . . . that where I am, there ye may be also' [John 14:2–3]? If you loved Me when you could not see Me except by faith, love Me more now when we have really become co-heirs of the Father. Come to Me with all that perplexes or gladdens. Come to the Elder Brother always waiting to receive you with joy."

Then He drew me to a seat and conversed with me long and earnestly, unfolding many of the mysteries of the divine life. I hung upon His words. I drank in every tone of His voice. I watched eagerly every line of the beloved face. And I was exalted, uplifted, upborne beyond the power of words to express. At length, with a divine smile, He arose.

"We will often meet," He said. And I, bending over,

pressed my lips reverently to the hand still clasping my own. Then laying His hands a moment in blessing upon my bowed head, He passed noiselessly and swiftly from the house.

As I stood watching the Savior's fast-receding figure passing beneath the flower-laden trees, I saw two beautiful young girls approaching the way He went. With arms intertwining they came, happily conversing together, sweet Mary Bates and Mae Camden. When they saw the master, they flew to meet Him with a glad cry. He joyously extended a hand to each. They turned and, each clinging to His hands, one upon either side, they accompanied Him on His way.

Looking up trustingly into His face as He talked with them, they were apparently conversing with Him with happy freedom. I saw His face from time to time in profile, as He turned and looked down lovingly, first upon one, then the other lovely, upturned face. I thought, *That is the way He would have us be with Him—really as children with a beloved elder brother.*

---

"For the Lamb at the center of the throne will be their shepherd; he will lead them to springs of living water. And God will wipe away every tear from their eyes."

Revelation 7:17

# The Doors of Heaven
## *Betty Malz*

As Betty Malz lay dying in the Union Hospital in Terre Haute, Indiana, the Lord awakened her father, the Rev. Glenn Perkins, at 3:30 in the morning and told him to take the forty-minute drive back to the hospital. It was part of God's master plan that Betty's father be standing by his daughter's bed to see for himself the drama about to take place. He arrived to find that all like supports had been removed and a sheet placed over her head. This story is told in her book *My Glimpse of Eternity*.

---

It must have been sometime around five A.M. when my body functions apparently stopped, much as they had earlier in the day. Only this time there was no one at my bedside to call for the emergency equipment.

The transition was serene and peaceful. I was walking up a beautiful green hill. It was steep, but my leg motion was effortless and a deep ecstasy flooded my body. Despite three incisions in my body from the operations, I stood erect without pain, enjoying my tallness, free from inhibitions about it. I looked down. I seemed to be barefoot, but the complete outer shape of my body was a blur and colorless. Yet I was walking on grass, the most vivid shade of green I had ever seen. Each blade was perhaps one inch long, the texture, like fine velvet; every blade was vibrant and moving. As the bottoms of my feet touched the grass, something alive in the grass was transmitted up through my whole body with each step I took.

*Can this be death?* I wondered. If so, I certainly had nothing to fear. There was no darkness, no uncertainty, only a change in location and a total sense of well-being.

All around me was a magnificent deep blue sky, unobscured by clouds. Looking about, I realized that there was no road or path. Yet I seemed to know where to go.

Then I realized that I was not walking alone. To the left, and a little behind me, strode a tall, masculine-looking figure in a robe. I wondered if he was an angel and tried to see if he had wings. But he was facing me and I could not see his back. I sensed, however, that he could go anywhere he wanted and very quickly.

We did not speak to each other. Somehow it didn't seem necessary, for we were both going in the same direction. Then I became aware that he was not a stranger. He knew me and I felt a strange kinship with him. Where had we met? Had we always known each other? It seemed we had. Where were we now going?

As we walked together I saw no sun—but light was everywhere. Off to the left there were multicolored flowers blooming. Also trees, shrubs. On the right was a low stone wall.

Once years before I had climbed to the top of Logan's Pass in Glacier National Park, breathing the pure, clean, unused air amidst the snowcapped peaks. There were small flowers blooming even in the snow. My legs had been sore and tired from that climb.

This climb was different. My legs were not tired and I wasn't aware of any temperature. There was no snow though I seemed to be in a high altitude. There seemed to be no seasons but it felt like early spring. My emotion was a combination of feelings: youth, serenity, fulfillment, health, awareness, tranquility. I felt I had everything I ever wanted to have. I was everything I had ever intended to be. I was arriving at where I had always dreamed of being.

The wall to my right was higher now and made of many-colored, multi-tiered stones. A light from the other side of the wall shone through a long row of amber-colored gems several feet above my head. *Topaz,* I thought to myself. . . .

Just as we crested the top of the hill I heard my father's voice calling, "Jesus, Jesus, Jesus." His voice was a long distance away. I thought about turning back to find him. I did not because I knew my destination was ahead. We walked along in silence save for the whisper of a gentle breeze ruffling the white, sheer garments of the angel.

We came upon a magnificent, silver structure. It was like a palace except there were no towers. As we walked toward it I heard voices. They were melodious, harmonious, blending in chorus and I heard the word *Jesus.* There were more than four parts to their harmony. I not only heard the singing and felt the singing but I joined the singing. I have always had a girl's body, but a boy's low voice. Suddenly I realized I was singing the way I had always wanted to . . . in high, clear and sweet tones. . . .

While the angel and I walked together I sensed we could go wherever we willed ourselves to go and be there instantly. Communication between us was through the projection of thoughts. The choirs began a new chorus, sung in four parts and different languages. The words were understandable, but I don't know how or why. We all seemed to be on some universal wavelength. I thought at the time, *I will never forget the melody and these words.* But later I could recall only two: *Jesus* and *redeemed.*

The angel stepped forward and put the palm of his hand upon a gate, which I had not noticed before. About twelve feet high, the gate was a solid sheet of pearl, with no handles. . . . The atmosphere inside was somehow filtered through. My feeling was of ecstatic joy and anticipation at the thought of going inside.

When the angel stepped forward, pressing his palm on the gate, an opening appeared in the center of the pearl panel and slowly widened and deepened as though the translucent material was dissolving. Inside I saw what appeared to be a street of golden color with an overlay of glass or water. The yellow light that appeared was dazzling. There is no way to describe it. I saw no figure, yet I was conscious of a Person. Suddenly I knew that the light was Jesus, the Person was Jesus.

I did not have to move. The light was all about me. There seemed to be some heat in it as if I were standing in sunlight; my body began to glow. Every part of me was absorbing the light. I felt bathed by the rays of a powerful, penetrating, loving energy.

The angel looked at me and communicated the thought: *Would you like to go in and join them?*

I longed with all my being to go inside, yet I hesitated. Did I have a choice? Then I remembered my father's voice. Perhaps I should go and find him.

"I would like to stay and sing a little longer, then go back down the hill," I finally answered. I started to say something more. But it was too late.

The gates slowly melted into one sheet of pearl again and we began walking back down the same beautiful hill. This time the jeweled wall was on my left and the angel walked on my right. . . .

After my descent I slowed down and stopped. . . . I was back in my hospital bed now and letters in the light flashing before me stretched all the way from the window, past my bed and on into the room. They read: *I am the resurrection and the life; he that believeth in me, though he were dead, yet shall he live.*

The words were so alive that they pulsated. I knew that I had to touch those living words. I reached up and out and pushed the sheet off my face. At that instant the Word of God literally became life to me. The warmth in the moving letters flowed into my fingers and up my arm. I sat up in bed! . . .

My father was staring at me in a state of shock. . . . He was stunned, too startled to cry out, or hug me, or shed tears of joy. Rather he was rooted to the spot, struck dumb with awe before the majesty of the working of God. . . .

The nurses wanted to put the tubes back in me but I shook my head. "I'm sure I don't need them anymore. I'm hungry. Please tell Dr. Bherne that I want some real food.". . .

There sure wasn't much left of me—just an emaciated yellowish-green face and a skinny disintegrated eighty-pound skeleton of a body. But how alive I felt!

---

The city does not need the sun or the moon to shine on it, for the glory of God gives it light, and the Lamb is its lamp. The nations will walk by its light, and the kings of the earth will bring their splendor into it.

Revelation 21:23–24

## Section 3

# To Make Disciples

# Paul Warned in Jerusalem

Paul, known before his conversion as Saul, met Jesus in a dramatic vision, recorded in Acts 9. The Lord continued to speak to him in dramatic and supernatural ways.

---

"When I returned to Jerusalem and was praying at the temple, I fell into a trance and saw the Lord speaking. 'Quick!' he said to me. 'Leave Jerusalem immediately, because they will not accept your testimony about me.'

" 'Lord,' I replied, 'these men know that I went from one synagogue to another to imprison and beat those who believe in you. And when the blood of your martyr Stephen was shed, I stood there giving my approval and guarding the clothes of those who were killing him.'

"Then the Lord said to me, 'Go; I will send you far away to the Gentiles.' " Acts 22:17–21

# The Fields Are White Unto Harvest
## Lillian Wiley

Lillian Wiley, wife of the late Dr. Kenneth Wiley, was a Bible teacher and president of the Oak Park, Illinois, Women's Aglow chapter.

For more than several years I had heard Jesus saying, "The fields are white unto harvest, but the laborers are few." He showed me white fields of harvest over and over again. I would awaken at night and see in the darkness of the room those words in shining white letters: *The fields are white unto harvest.*

We lived in the foothills of the San Gabriel mountains in San Dimas, California. One morning while driving to work I had a vision of Jesus in those mountains. I saw Him standing on a high mountain gazing across that huge valley. Mount Baldy of that mountain range is more than eight thousand feet high and Jesus towered above that.

The foot of that great basin is populated by many cities and thousands of homes. His arms were outstretched over that vast metropolitan area and there was such sadness on His face. He turned and looked right at me and said, "Where are My laborers?"

Something drew my attention to His right. I saw a large white clock outlined in black with black numerals and black hands. The hands were set at five minutes to twelve. One more time He turned to me and said with tears running down His face, "The laborers are so few!"

This vision occurred many years ago and I *still* hear the words *The fields are white unto harvest, but the laborers are few.* And I hear this as well: "The harvest is past, the summer has ended, and we are not saved" (Jeremiah 8:20).

Over the years I have had several visions of Jesus and one has occurred several times. It always seems to come during a time of intense prayer, sometimes while I am alone, other times when a group is interceding. It is always the same.

Jesus is coming swiftly from the heavens in a mass of billowing, swirling clouds. It looks as though a great storm is following Him, but I feel no wind. His great robe billows and swirls around His feet.

He is coming with such intentness and swiftness that it is almost frightening, yet I cannot take my eyes from Him. His eyes look straight ahead, as though they are going to the heart of the situation or problem. Those eyes are penetrating and fierce and fill me with awe.

Like a bolt of lightning He comes and stands above the person or group in prayer. And then He is gone!

He told them, "The harvest is plentiful, but the workers are few. Ask the Lord of the harvest, therefore, to send out workers into his harvest field."   Luke 10:2

# Heaven and the Angels
## *General William Booth*

William Booth (1829–1912), founder and leader of the Salvation Army, was born in England and converted while still young.

It was when he was allowed to see a vision of some of the marshaled hosts of heaven that William Booth became deeply concerned about the poverty of the lower classes in England and devoted himself to the poor and homeless.

An early street-corner preacher and later an ordained Methodist New Connexion minister, he preached, averaging two sermons a day, almost until the time of his death. In 1890 he published his great book, *In Darkest England On the Way Out.*

What a sight that was! Worth toiling a lifetime to behold it! Nearest the King were the patriarchs and apostles of ancient time. Next, rank after rank, came the holy martyrs who had died for Him. Then came the army of warriors who had fought for Him in every part of the world; and around and about, above and below, I beheld myriads of spirits who were never heard of outside their own neighborhoods, or beyond their own times, who with self-denying zeal and untiring toil had labored to extend God's Kingdom and to save the souls of men.

Encircling this gorgeous scene above, beneath, around, hovered glittering angelic beings who had kept their first estate—proud, it seemed to me, to minister to the happiness and exultation of those redeemed out of the poor world whence I came.

I was bewildered by the scene. The songs, the music, the shouts of the multitude came like the roar of a thousand cataracts, echoed and re-echoed through the glory-lit mountains, and the magnificent and endless army of happy spirits ravished my senses with passionate delight.

[Then the King addressed General Booth who, until that time, had lived a lazy, "professing" Christian life:]

"Thou wilt feel thyself little in harmony with these—once the companions of My tribulation and now of My glory—who counted not their lives dear unto themselves in order to bring honor to Me and salvation to men." And He gave a look of admiration at the host of apostles and martyrs and warriors gathered around Him.

Oh, that look of Jesus! I felt that to have one such loving recognition would be worth dying a hundred deaths at the stake, worth being torn asunder by wild beasts. The angelic escort felt it, too, for their responsive burst of praise shook the very skies and the ground on which I lay.

Then the King turned His eyes on me again. How I wished that some mountain would fall upon me and hide me forever from His presence! But I wished in vain. Some invisible and irresistible force compelled me to look up, and my eyes met His once more. I felt, rather than heard, Him saying to me in words that engaged themselves as fire upon my brain: "Go back to earth. I will give thee another opportunity. Prove thyself worthy of My name. Show to the world that thou possessest My Spirit by doing My work and becoming, on My behalf, a savior of men.

"Thou shalt return hither [to heaven] when thou hast finished the battle, and I will give thee a place in My conquering train and a share in My glory."

---

Then he said to them all: "If anyone would come after me, he must deny himself and take up his cross daily and follow me. For whoever wants to save his life will lose it, but whoever loses his life for me will save it. What good is it for a man to gain the whole world, and yet lose or forfeit his very self? If anyone is ashamed of me and my words, the Son of Man will be ashamed of him when he comes in his glory and in the glory of the Father and of the holy angels."

Luke 9:23–26

# Blessed Aleyde
## Fr. M. Raymond

In the middle of the thirteenth century Sister Aleyde entered the Convent of La Cambre, near Brussels, at the age of seven. After years of devoted service in the convent, Aleyde became ill. The physician told her that she had leprosy and would have to live in a cell.

---

Aleyde was astonished by the announcement that she was a leper, and hence was keener in her perception than usual. She saw the fear in the eyes of all; she noted the shrinking away of even the bravest and efforts of others to avoid her very presence. She was somewhat bewildered by it all but tried to be as kind and generous in her thoughts as she could. Still, she was human enough to feel hurt by their actions. . . .

The cell was built. The little nun was led to it. She entered with a smile on her somewhat distorted face and kept her promise: She was not afraid. And the Christ who could not resist the faith of the leper who prostrated herself saying, "Lord, if Thou wilt . . . ," nor the plea of those who cried, "Master, mercy . . . " was so touched by this trust of the Belgian nun that He appeared to her, smiled, and said:

"Aleyde, you will never want, I shall be your Cellarer."
When we realize that the cellarer, according to St. Bene-
dict's rule, is he who provides everything the brethren may
need, we can see why the little leper knew she had received
something better than a cure. . . .

Aleyde had insisted that she be awakened at midnight
[before Easter Sunday] so that she might assist at the celebration of the Resurrection. The heroic Sister who attended her agreed and, after arousing her, helped her to a
prie-dieu. Through the open windows of the church and
into the tiny cell came the happy chant of the Easter Alle-
luias.

The Office moved on and the lessons were being sung
when the attendant noticed the little leper shift her position
on the prie-dieu. This was exceptional, for Aleyde's knees
were so sick and sore that any movement was excruciating.
Suddenly the chant of the responsory Surrexit Dominus de
Sepulchro . . . was begun. Aleyde's eyes, sunk deep in dark
sockets and looking like pools of fire, seemed to open wider
and wider.

The attendant followed their gaze and saw the sky above
them open like some great curtain, while light, as from the
face of some fiery furnace, sprouted down upon the convent, setting every building brilliantly aglow. The Sister
attendant cried out in fright. Aleyde made a quiet gesture
with what remained of her right hand, which told the nun
not to be scared. Then the small cell drank in, as it were,
the torrent of celestial light, and the mystery that the responsory told about became plain to the Sister attendant.
Christ, the Risen and Glorified, had come to visit the soul

of one who was as white as snow not only physically, but also spiritually.

As Easter Week moved on Aleyde's state became more and more agonizing. Once when the pain squeezed a cry from her, the attendant was greatly moved.

"Sister," said the attendant, "I have often heard you lament the length of your exile. I know your longing for heaven. I also know something of the agonies you endure. Tell me, please, that what you said to me the first day I came to you is not true. Tell me that you will not live after me; that you will not suffer much more."

Aleyde showed her gratitude in her expression for such genuine sympathy but made no reply. It was only later in the day that she turned to the Sister and said: "Sister dear, what I told you that first day is true. You will die before me, and you will go straight to God. You must then help me even more than you do now for Jesus has told me that the sufferings of these past years are as nothing compared to what I will yet suffer."

"Oh!" cried the attendant. "How can that be! How could God ask so much!"

Aleyde's sunken eyes lit with that smile that could not brighten any other feature but her eyes, so far had the leprosy progressed.

"And you can smile at such a prospect!" exclaimed the attendant.

"It is a happiness," replied the leper. "It is a great happiness to help God. Jesus has told me that there are certain souls that cannot be saved—cannot be saved, mind you— unless I suffer. That is why I am glad to remain here after you have gone. That is why I am happy that this body of mine can serve the Christ. But never forget what I said. You must help me from heaven. I do not like pain!"

---

Now I rejoice in what was suffered for you, and I fill up in my flesh what is still lacking in regard to Christ's afflictions, for the sake of his body, which is the church.                                             Colossians 1:24

# Different Worlds
## *Dharam Singh*

In the words of Dharam Singh: "I was born a Hindu and I intended to die a Hindu—until I came to know Jesus and let His power change me."

---

My great-great-great-great-grandfather came from East India to the Fiji Islands, bringing with him centuries of culture, custom and the Hindu religion. My father was a Hindu priest and wanted his son to follow in his footsteps, so my childhood in the Fiji Islands was in the strictest Hindu tradition.

My mother was a devout sun-worshiper. I adopted her beliefs also until my first year of high school. In geography class one day the teacher was talking about the sun. The dictionary told me that the sun is a body of great mass in space.

As I walked home from school that afternoon, I looked up at the sun and for the first time realized that it wasn't a god.

"Sun," I said, "you are just a sun and not my god. From this day on I will not worship you."

I began to study other Far Eastern religions, especially Buddhism and Islam. Throughout my childhood I had heard the witness of Christians, but I rejected everything they said, and if someone gave me an article or tract about Christianity I burned it immediately. Something in me didn't want to know the Lord Jesus—yet I believe He always had His hand upon me.

After getting the best education the Fiji government could give, I emigrated to Canada in 1959, intending to become a doctor. But as I had to earn the money first, I took a job in a logging camp, hoping to save enough money to go back to school.

Gradually I became an alcoholic and I lost all respect for myself. When I realized I would never get back to the university, I sank into depression. . . .

I met and married Nydia, a beautiful Filipino schoolteacher. During our honeymoon in New York City, I went to a Christian church for the first time in my life. There I picked up a tract that said Hindus worship cows and monkeys and elephants. It made me angry.

Although I had left the logging camp, I clung to its lifestyle and dragged Nydia down with me. But then Nydia began to act very strangely. She became more pleasant to live with. She didn't get mad at me anymore, no matter how drunk I was when I came home. Searching for something called the baptism in the Holy Spirit, she had gone to a Pentecostal church, had turned her life over to Jesus, and had been "filled with the Holy Ghost."

One day in 1971 the pastor of the church Nydia attended came to visit. "Dharam," he told me, "you need Jesus."

"I was born a Hindu, and I will die a Hindu. I have all the booze I need and I'm happy as I am. I don't need your God. I'm not interested in your Jesus!"

He never did preach to me again, but instead let me see Jesus in his life. Surprisingly we became the best of friends. Later, when he invited me to his church, I agreed to come.

During one Sunday morning service, fast asleep as usual, I was suddenly jolted awake. A man in the church, his face aglow, was speaking out loud in a foreign language.

When he had finished and sat down someone else stood and gave what seemed to be an interpretation of what the man had said. It was all about the Holy Spirit encouraging the Church.

I was astounded. I had seen "miracles" in Hinduism where people walked on fire and carried more than a ton of weight by themselves, and I knew about spirits, but I didn't know that there was a "spirit" in Christianity.

Later that day the minister's wife went over the second chapter of Acts with me and explained all the gifts the Holy Spirit has given to the Church.

One night I began to worship Him. I felt my whole body being engulfed by the power of His love. I asked Him, "Is heaven real? And am I really saved?" The Lord showed me a vision of heaven's gates and the Book of Life. When I asked the pastor about my vision, he confirmed it from the Bible.

I began to seek the Lord in earnest, asking what my ministry was to be. One evening as I prayed I had a vision of Jesus. He stood in midair with His hands extended. Millions of people ran toward Him; the crowd stretched as far as I could see. The Holy Spirit said to me, "You are going to be a soulwinner for Me."

From that day on the Word of God came alive to me, and I have been winning souls for Jesus wherever I go.

---

I want you to know, brothers, that the gospel I preached is not something that man made up. I did not receive it from any man, nor was I taught it; rather, I received it by revelation from Jesus Christ. For you have heard of my previous way of life in Judaism, how intensely I persecuted the church of God and tried to destroy it. I was advancing in Judaism beyond many Jews of my own age and was extremely zealous for the traditions of my fathers. But when God, who set me apart from birth and called me by his grace, was pleased to reveal his Son in me so that I might preach him among the Gentiles . . . I went immediately.        Galatians 1:11–17

# The Rising of My Soul
## Charles G. Finney

During the year 1857–1858, the Lord guided Charles G. Finney in winning more than one hundred thousand persons to Christ. The Holy Spirit impressed those consciences with the necessity of holy living in such a way as to obtain lasting results. Research shows that 85 percent of Finney's converts remained true to God. This account describes his initial experience with God. He and Squire Wright were moving books and furniture to another office. . . .

My mind remained in that profoundly tranquil state. There was a great sweetness and tenderness in my thoughts and feelings. Everything appeared to be going right, and nothing seemed to disturb me or ruffle me in the least. . . .

Just before evening the thought took possession of my mind, that as soon as I was left alone in the new office, I would try to pray again—that I was not going to abandon the subject of religion and give it up, at any rate. . . . Just at dark Squire W——, seeing that everying was adjusted, bade me good night. . . . As I closed the door and turned around, my heart seemed to be liquid within me. All my feelings seemed to rise and flow out; and the utterance of my heart was, "I want to pour my whole soul out to God." The rising of my soul was so great that I rushed into the room back of the front office to pray.

There was no fire and no light in the room; nevertheless, it appeared to me as if it were perfectly light. As I went in and shut the door after me, it seemed as if I met the Lord Jesus Christ face to face. It did not occur to me then, nor did it for some time afterward, that it was wholly a mental state. On the contrary it seemed to me that I saw Him as I would see any other man. He said nothing, but looked at me in such a manner as to break me right down at His feet. I have always since regarded this as a most remarkable state of mind; for it seemed to me a reality, that He stood before me, and I fell down at His feet and poured out my soul to Him. I wept aloud like a child, and made such confession as I could with my choked utterance. It seemed to me that I bathed His feet with my tears; and yet I had no distinct impression that I touched Him that I recollect.

I must have continued in this state for a good while; but my mind was too much absorbed with the interview to recollect anything that I said. But I know, as soon as my mind became calm enough to break off from the interview, I returned to the front office and found that the fire I had made of large wood was nearly burned out. But as I turned and was about to take a seat by the fire, I received a mighty baptism of the Holy Ghost. Without any expectation of it, without ever having the thought in my mind that there was any such thing for me, without any recollection that I had ever heard the thing mentioned by any person in the world, the Holy Ghost descended on me in a manner that seemed to go through me, body and soul. I could feel the impression, like a wave of electricity, going through and through me. Indeed it seemed to come in waves and waves of liquid love; for I could not express it in any other way. It seemed like the very breath of God. I can recollect distinctly that it seemed to fan me, like immense wings.

No words can express the wonderful love that was shed abroad in my heart. I wept aloud with joy and love; and I do not know but I should say I literally bellowed out the unutterable gushings of my heart. The waves came over me and over me, one after the other, until I recollect I cried out, . . . "Lord, I cannot bear any more."

---

And when the centurion, who stood there in front of Jesus, heard his cry and saw how he died, he said, "Surely this man was the Son of God!"

Mark 15:39

# The Commission
## *Alem-la Meren*

In 1976 Alem-la Meren and her pastor-husband, Alem Meren, were participating in a revival meeting in the village of Chuchuyimlong in Nagaland, India. At the close of the evening when the crowds had left, they joined with a small group of believers to thank the Lord for His mighty outpouring of blessing during the meeting.

Alem-la narrated this story in their Naga tongue, while Pastor Alem interpreted. He spoke each phrase in somewhat broken English, very slowly, and with great awe—as though hearing it himself for the first time.

---

Suddenly a man appeared. He was different from all human men I had ever seen. He was very beautiful. His face had a different structure. I had never seen a man like this, even in a magazine picture. Who was He? I was very surprised.

At first I thought His clothing was glittering. I soon realized that a combination of green, white and rose light was coming from His body. I didn't see His whole figure. Just from the waist up. While wondering who this was, a cross appeared. He leaned against it, as though to testify He was Jesus.

I asked, "If You are the real Jesus, show me the nail prints."

He lowered His hands, turning the palms enough for me to see the print of the nails.

When I saw the marks in His hands, I knew for certain He was Jesus. He was very beautiful. Very beautiful.

I could sense an overwhelming humility coming from Him. Yet there was a strange thing in His face. It was something I could not understand for a long time. I saw a burden and a great dissatisfaction. It troubled me for many days. I asked the Lord repeatedly why His face was filled with such a burden.

Finally the interpretation came. The Lord spoke this to me: "I gave My life for all mankind. I paid the price for all men. But still many people are going to hell, and even more will go there. I am not happy because of that. You are happy and rejoicing because you have been touched by My Spirit. But I am not happy because so many are going to hell!"

My heart melted and my eyes filled with tears at that moment. I began to feel His tremendous burden for souls. It was then that I decided to commit the rest of my life totally to the cause of bringing the lost to Jesus Christ.

---

Then Jesus came to them and said, "All authority in heaven and on earth has been given to me. Therefore go and make disciples of all nations, baptizing them in the name of the Father and of the Son and of the Holy Spirit, and teaching them to obey everything I have commanded you. And surely I will be with you always, to the very end of the age."

Matthew 28:18–20

*Section 4*

# Yielded

# Daniel and the Lord's Messenger

Daniel was taken to Babylon by Nebuchadnezzar in 605 B.C. with other young men of nobility—"handsome, well informed and quick to understand." When he and his companions remained true to their faith, refusing to partake of the idolatries of the pagan kings, God rewarded them with great learning and bestowed on Daniel the gifts of visions and dream interpretation.

---

On the twenty-fourth day of the first month, as I was standing on the bank of the great river, the Tigris, I looked up and there before me was a man dressed in linen, with a belt of the finest gold around his waist. His body was like chrysolite, his face like lightning, his eyes like flaming torches, his arms and legs like the gleam of burnished bronze, and his voice like the sound of a multitude.

I, Daniel, was the only one who saw the vision; the men with me did not see it, but such terror overwhelmed them that they fled and hid themselves. So I was left alone, gazing at this great vision; I had no strength left, my face turned deathly pale and I was helpless. Then I heard him speaking, and as I listened to him, I fell into a deep sleep, my face to the ground.

A hand touched me and set me trembling on my hands and knees. He said, "Daniel, you who are highly esteemed, consider carefully the words I am about to speak to you, and stand up, for I have now been sent to you." And when he said this to me, I stood up trembling.

Then he continued, "Do not be afraid, Daniel. Since the first day that you set your mind to gain understanding and to humble yourself before your God, your words were heard, and I have come in response to them."

Daniel 10:4–12

# His Open Arms
## *Commander Carl Wilgus*

As a young naval officer, Commander Carl Wilgus found the joy and thrill of the new birth. As he says, "I had heard the story of Jesus many times, and I thought I was a Christian. Then one Sunday morning in a little country church I heard it anew, and God opened my spiritual eyes and unstopped my spiritual ears. I was not seeking Jesus that Sunday morning; but someone had been praying, and He was seeking me."

At the close of the service an invitation was given for sinners to give their lives to Christ. I looked around at the congregation and told myself I was as good as anyone there and no one had better invite me to go forward. I made up my mind that if that happened, I was going out the back door.

When no person could help me find salvation, the Holy Spirit gave the personal invitation! The presence of the Lord was there with such power that I began to tremble. He gave me a choice: "Christ, or a cocktail glass. You choose this day." I couldn't resist His invitation to accept Christ as my Savior, so I went forward and fell on my knees at the altar, overwhelmed at His concern for and knowledge of me. That moment a peace came into my heart that has continually flooded my soul ever since, even in times of danger and trial—and there have been several such times.

One of them occurred several years ago while flying a four-engine aircraft from an airfield in Florida. I was an Ensign plane commander at the time and pilot of the aircraft.

We had just taken off from the airfield when the number two engine blew the exhaust stack loose, allowing flames to enter the nacelle area where fuel, oil lines and oil tanks were located. We quickly reduced power on that engine and continued climbing on the three good ones. The aircraft was quite heavy and we were still very low, so we did not stop the engine completely by "feathering" the propeller into the wind. Instead, we closed its throttle and set full low rpm to allow minimum drag.

The other three engines were getting hot as we climbed a few hundred feet and turned back toward the airfield. Suddenly the number one engine "seized" internally and stopped completely. The propeller was turning so fast, however, that all the nose section bolts sheared. Oil ran back on the red-hot exhaust stacks setting the whole engine on fire. I ordered, "Feather number one!" and reached for the throttles to get maximum power. The plane was dropping so fast I realized we couldn't clear the trees immediately below. To myself I said, *So this is how I'm going to die!* There wasn't a doubt in my mind but that I had just flown my last mile.

At that instant I had a vision: Jesus was standing with arms outstretched waiting for me. I remembered that my name was written in the Lamb's Book of Life—that I was a child of God. A feeling of peace, joy and sheer ecstasy swept over me.

I saw another figure standing there, sideways to me. I recognized him immediately as Death, but his hands, which were behind his back, were bound together. Death could not touch me and the Lord was waiting for me with open arms!

I cried out, "Jesus, save us!" That huge airplane sailed over the tree tops and did not crash. I don't know how—only that it was the Lord.

We were now so low I planned to ditch the plane in the ocean near shore, but unaccountably it continued to hold some altitude and airspeed. We were just clearing the wave tops when I saw an unused runway that was too short for the big planes and was closed to all aircraft. We turned quickly, landed safely and were able to stop at the very end of the runway.

Our God is able to do anything!

---

I sought the Lord, and he answered me; he delivered me from all my fears. Those who look to him are radiant; their faces are never covered with shame. This poor man called, and the Lord heard him; he saved him out of all his troubles.     Psalm 34:4–6

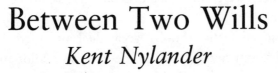

# Between Two Wills
## *Kent Nylander*

Pastor Kent Nylander has been in the ministry for more than twenty years and is presently serving Grace Lutheran Church in Bensenville, Illinois.

---

I had been raised in the church. My parents took me every Sunday and they didn't accept any excuses. I knew that it was the thing to do, but in my heart I wasn't seeking the Lord. Our church was pastored by faithful men; yet I cannot recall a single sermon with the exception of one preached by a visiting son of the congregation not long after he was ordained.

It wasn't until my college years that I began to ask questions. I wondered about the reality of it all . . . if the Gospel message was true . . . how Christ who lived on earth some two thousand years ago could be the power for life and salvation in our generation. I began to read the Scriptures on my own for the first time and, though I had not turned to the Lord with my whole heart, I felt His call on my life.

After graduation from college I entered the Navy, and during some of those long watches at night in the Combat Information Center aboard ship, I continued to read my Bible during times of inactivity. I knew then that I was being given a call to enter the ministry; but I had other plans for my future: My dream was to fly. Before long my orders were cut and I was on my way to Pensacola, Florida.

I enjoyed flight school a great deal and there I determined to put twenty years in the Navy as a pilot and then enter seminary. And all the while the tension increased, the warfare between two wills—mine and the Lord's. Finally one day I walked into the office of the administration at the school and resigned.

"Not my will, but Thine be done." That was to be my struggle. The Lord had clearly shown me that nothing would be satisfying in life but to follow Him faithfully, and how true that has proven to be. But I was one who stubbornly wanted my own will.

And then, suddenly in a moment, everything changed. In a dream it seemed as if I were standing on the grounds of the university I had attended. At the crest of the hill appeared One who shone with brilliance and authority. He said nothing but beckoned for me to come to Him. I felt as if I had exploded with joy and revelation.

Moments later, I found myself in what appeared to be the hall of the main building standing at the door of one of the rooms. At the back of the room people were standing, conversing with one another. In the middle of the room, sitting alone on a chair, with head lowered, sat the Christ I had seen shortly before. He appeared to be saddened and lonely. I knew instinctively that we were gathered there in His name, yet no one sat at His feet. I stood in the hall pointing Him out to everyone who passed by, but I did not go in to Him myself. It was some years later, after I had been in the ministry for three years, that I came to understand that vision. . . .

I had been preaching and teaching without really knowing Him in a personal way; I had never truly asked Him to live in my heart. I had represented Him without seeking intimacy with Him and, thus, my ministry had caused the people gathered in His name just to stand around, not sit at His feet. That was the fruit of an unresolved struggle between my will and the Lord's. When I finally did surrender to Him, the hymn "I Have Decided to Follow Jesus" played over and over again in my head for three days.

---

As Jesus and his disciples were on their way, he came to a village where a woman named Martha opened her home to him. She had a sister called Mary, who sat at the Lord's feet listening to what he said. But Martha was distracted by all the preparations that had to be made. She came to him and asked, "Lord, don't you care that my sister has left me to do the work by myself? Tell her to help me!"

"Martha, Martha," the Lord answered, "you are worried and upset about many things, but only one thing is needed. Mary has chosen what is better, and it will not be taken away from her."

Luke 10:38–42

❦

# A Changed Life
## *Dorothy Adams*

Dorothy Adams, a licensed practical nurse, is an active member of the Austin Messiah Lutheran Church in Chicago.

---

When I moved to the west side of Chicago in 1979, little did I know how much my life was going to change. When I decided to send my children to Sunday school, the Lord began working in my life. From my past experience with church, I refused to hear Him. I was to soon learn that God's plans are not to be ignored.

Having three children and going to school full-time, I was often awake in the early hours of the morning. One of those times I was startled to see a scene appear suddenly before me.

There stood Jesus. As if suspended in midair with outstretched arms, He was calling His children to Him. I looked and saw that many people were coming to the Lord. I was outside the crowd, looking for myself among the children of God. I searched for what seemed like hours but was unable to find myself. Then the image was gone just as suddenly as it had appeared.

I knew from that moment on that my life would never be the same. The Lord had revealed to me where I stood in relation to Him. He gave me the chance of a lifetime, an eternal lifetime, to claim the salvation of Calvary.

That night I read the first two verses of Psalm 138: "I will praise you, O Lord, with all my heart; before the 'gods' I will sing your praise. I will bow down toward your holy temple and will praise your name for your love and your faithfulness, for you have exalted above all things your name and your word."

---

As a shepherd looks after his scattered flock when he is with them, so will I look after my sheep. I will rescue them from all the places where they were scattered on a day of clouds and darkness.

Ezekiel 34:12

# Taken by Surprise
## *John Wesley*

John Wesley, founder of Methodism, was born at Ep-
worth Rectory June 17, 1703. In 1738 Wesley found great
faith at a meeting in Aldersgate Street in London, where "I
found my heart strangely warmed." He traveled about eight
thousand miles a year by horseback in his preaching circuit
seldom preaching fewer than 5,000 times a year. This is
taken from his journals.

I talked largely with Ann Thorne and two others who
had been several times in trances. What they all agreed in
was 1) that when they went away, as they termed it, it was
always at the time they were fullest of the love of God; 2)
that it came upon them in a moment, without any previous
notice, and took away all their senses and strength; 3) that
there were some exceptions, but in general, from that moment, they were in another world, knowing nothing of
what was done or said by all that were around them.

About five in the afternoon I heard them singing hymns.
Soon after, Mr. Bee came up and told me Alice Miller
(fifteen years old) had fallen into a trance. . . . I do not
know whether I ever saw a human face look so beautiful;

sometimes it was covered with a smile, as from joy, mixing with love and reverence; but the tears fell still while not so fast. Her pulse was quite regular. In about a half an hour I observed her countenance change into the form of fear, pity and distress; then she burst into a flood of tears and cried out, "Dear Lord, they will be damned!" But in about five minutes her smiles returned, and only love and joy appeared in her face.

About seven her senses returned. I asked, "Where have you been?"

"I have been with my Savior."

"In heaven or on earth?"

"I cannot tell; but I was in glory."

. . . Before I left Glasgow I heard so strange an account that I desired to hear it from the person himself. He was a sexton and yet for many years had little troubled himself about religion. I set down his words and leave every man to form his own judgment upon them.

"Sixteen weeks ago I was walking, an hour before sunset, behind the high kirk; and, looking on one side, I saw one close to me who looked in my face and asked me how I did. I answered, 'Pretty well.' He said, 'You have had many troubles; but how have you improved them?' He then told me all that I ever did; yea, and the thoughts that had been in my heart, adding, 'Be ready for My Second Coming.' And He was gone I knew not how. I trembled all over, and had no strength in me; but sank down to the ground. From that time I groaned continually under the load of sin, till at the Lord's Supper it was all taken away."

I know a man in Christ who fourteen years ago was caught up to the third heaven. Whether it was in the body or out of the body I do not know—God knows. And I know that this man . . . was caught up to Paradise. He heard inexpressible things, things that man is not permitted to tell.     2 Corinthians 12:2–4

The woman went back to the town and said to the people, "Come, see a man who told me everything I ever did. Could this be the Christ?"     John 4:28–29

# The Question
## *John Bunyan*

John Bunyan (1628–1688), author of *Pilgrim's Progress*, was a part of the Puritan movement, which took it for granted that a person would suffer for all the things he believed were right. During a time of political chaos he chose to be imprisoned for twelve years rather than compromise his moral beliefs.

Bunyan was a rural tinker when he experienced conversion. There is plenty of evidence in his writings that the spring of his imagination was the Bible. It was actually when he was married (at age 22) and a baby daughter was born blind that real change came into his life. This great

change happened on a Sunday afternoon while he was playing tipcat with friends. . . .

---

A voice did suddenly dart from heaven into my soul,
which said, *Wilt thou leave thy sins, and go to heaven? or
have thy sins, and go to hell?* At this I was put to an
exceeding maze; wherefore, leaving my cat upon the
ground, I looked up to heaven, and was as if I had with the
eyes of my understanding, seen the Lord Jesus looking
down upon me, as being very hotly displeased with me,
and as if He did severely threaten me with some grievous
punishment for these, and other ungodly practices.

---

The Lord will rescue me from every evil attack and
will bring me safely to his heavenly kingdom. To him
be glory for ever and ever. Amen.   2 Timothy 4:18

# The Glory of God
*Frances Hunter*

Frances Hunter and her husband, Charles, are renowned
speakers and writers. This is taken from their book *His
Power Through You.*

Just as Jesus appeared to Paul on the road to Damascus, He appeared in person to the group attending our Campmeeting '83. Those attending that service will never be the same again. It occurred during a time of praise and worship.

The dramatic appearance was preceded by a huge superwhite cloud on the stage, which covered the entire area and looked like a huge thunderhead in the sky. The glory and the presence of God were felt immediately; the very air seemed to be charged with electricity. There was a stillness and a holiness that you could almost reach out and touch. The effect was so awesome it was impossible to speak because to be in the presence of the Lord Jesus Christ is almost more than a human mind or body can stand.

After a few brief moments, He disappeared back into the glory cloud, and my heart cried out, *Jesus, come back! Come back! Don't go away.* He had literally melted into the glory of God and was not visible for any of us to see.

Suddenly, as quickly as He had disappeared, He seemed to walk back through the cloud of God's presence and was again visible. Our hearts raced with excitement and joy. The glory of the moment was short-lived, however, because once again He seemed to dissolve into the glory of God and was no longer visible. Again my inner being cried out, *Don't go away, Jesus! Don't go away. Come back!* No one who has beheld Jesus will ever want to depart from His presence. I knew He was there, but I couldn't see Him because He was hidden in God's glory.

His appearance and then His disappearance into the glory cloud continued for possibly twelve to fifteen minutes, and then God spoke. He said, "This is the way I want *you* to be. I want you to be so hidden in Him that the world will never see you; all they will see is My glory."

God wants us to be walking in the beauty of His holiness. He is calling on the Body of Christ to be so totally committed to Him that nothing else matters in our lives, to be so "in Him" that the world will see Jesus in us.

---

Glory in Christ Jesus, and . . . put no confidence in the flesh. Philippians 3:3

# F. B. Meyer and the Keys to Life
## Dr. Benjamin T. Browne

Dr. F. B. Meyer (1847–1929) of Christ Church, London, was a well-known Baptist clergyman at the turn of the century. He introduced Dwight L. Moody to the British churches, and from that time on was a lifelong friend of the American evangelist. Meyer's ministry focused on social, temperance and reclamation work, which led him into the political world. In addition, he wrote several books that continue in their popularity today.

---

Dr. F. B. Meyer of Christ Church, London, was seated one day in his study engaged in deep meditation. He was disturbed over the fact that his ministry seemed to be unfruitful and lacking in spiritual power. He was cast into deep spiritual concern and distress.

Suddenly Christ seemed to enter the room and stand beside him. "Let me have the key to your life," Christ said to him. The experience was so vivid that Meyer reached into his pocket to take out a bunch of keys.

"Are all the keys of your life here?" asked Jesus as He slowly examined the keys placed in His hands.

"Yes, Lord," said Meyer, "all the keys." Then with a sudden pang of conscience he added, "All the keys to the rooms in my life except one small room." There was still one place in his life where he was not willing to give Christ full and final control.

The Lord slowly handed the keys back to Meyer saying sadly, "If you cannot trust Me with all the keys to all the rooms in your life, I cannot accept any of the keys." Christ turned and started to walk out of the room.

Meyer said that in sudden alarm it came to him that Christ was somehow moving out of his life because he was shutting Him out from one of his interests. Meyer stood up and pleaded, "Come back to me, Lord. Come back to me and I will give You all the keys of my life. You can have this last key, too." Christ took all the keys of all the rooms of Meyer's life in His hand, smiled upon him and then vanished.

Dr. Meyer said that from that time forward blessed communion with Christ flowed through his life continually and sources of power and blessing were opened up that he had never dreamed of before.

---

Seek first his kingdom and his righteousness, and all these things will be given to you as well.

Matthew 6:33

## Section 5

# In Times of Trouble

# Ezekiel and God's Glory

During the Babylonian exile of the children of Israel, during which time they longed for Jerusalem and Temple worship, the prophet Ezekiel was given a vision of the new Jerusalem to come in the next world and the One who reigns there.

---

In the sixth year, in the sixth month on the fifth day, while I was sitting in my house and the elders of Judah were sitting before me, the hand of the Sovereign Lord came upon me there. I looked, and I saw a figure like that of a man. From what appeared to be his waist down he was like fire, and from there up his appearance was as bright as glowing metal. He stretched out what looked like a hand and took me by the hair of my head. The Spirit lifted me up between earth and heaven and in visions of God he took me to Jerusalem, to the entrance to the north gate of the inner court, where the idol that provokes to jealousy stood. And there before me was the glory of the God of Israel, as in the vision I had seen in the plain.

Ezekiel 8:1–4

# God's Plowman
## *Henry Krause*

Henry Krause, who went to be with the Lord in 1972, was president of the Krause Plow Corporation in Hutchinson, Kansas.

He built a successful business of manufacturing plows and gave more than a million dollars to God's work during his lifetime. He had many revelations and visions of Jesus.

---

One morning as Brother Krause was seated on the side of his bed he saw the Lord Jesus.

"He was dressed in a white robe with a red scarf over His shoulder. He had His left hand on His breast and His right hand extended to me. He stood and looked at me with eyes that seemed to burn clear through me.

"He never spoke a word. He didn't have to, for I stood in the presence of Him who is 'the Word of God' and knowledge began to pour into me. A new understanding and power of reasoning came into me. I was a totally different person. I understood people in a new way."

Again and again the Lord would come to Brother Krause in a dream or vision, especially when problems arose. God would teach him not only spiritual things but material things as well. He credited the Lord with giving him ideas for new designs in plows and other farming implements.

---

Observe what the Lord your God requires: Walk in his ways, and keep his decrees and commands, his laws and requirements, as written in the Law of Moses, so that you may prosper in all you do and wherever you go. 1 Kings 2:3

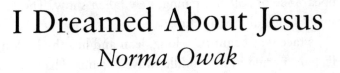

# I Dreamed About Jesus
## *Norma Owak*

Norma Owak lives in Orland Park, Illinois, and attends the Calvary Reformed Church there.

---

I had a dream several years ago in which I heard that Jesus was on the second floor of a warehouse-type building. The area was empty space and didn't even seem to have a ceiling.

I made my way anxiously up to where He was talking to a man. As I walked closer, Jesus turned as if He had been waiting for me and held out His arms slightly to greet me. All I could say was "Jesus, oh, Jesus." I had such joy within me and felt as though I would cry, but without tears. I sensed that He was waiting to see *me* and that He was intensely interested in *me*. His kindness and His reassurance about whatever I asked made my problems melt into nothing.

How did He look? He stood out like no one else. I was drawn to Him and could not take my eyes from His. I noticed other things about Him, but was drawn back to His eyes, which were blue.

He was graceful and tall and had a beautiful frame. His hands were large and handsome. He wore sandals and a white robe folded over without a belt. I was attracted by the material of the robe. There was no weave and it had the appearance of soft, glistening, new-fallen snow. The robe moved gracefully with Him.

His face was beautiful—long, lean and healthy looking. His hair, parted in the middle, waved against His face and had a soft radiance about it.

I couldn't help but love Him. Everything about Him was kindness and gentleness. He took all my concerns away.

---

Your attitude should be the same as that of Christ Jesus: Who . . . made himself nothing, taking the very nature of a servant, being made in human likeness. And being found in appearance as a man, he humbled himself and became obedient to death—even death on a cross! Therefore God exalted him to the highest place and gave him the name that is above every name, that at the name of Jesus every knee should bow, in heaven and on earth and under the earth.

Philippians 2:5–10

# The Hijacking
## *Kurt Carlson*

Kurt Carlson, a reserve officer in the U.S. Army Corps of Engineers, was called to active duty in the desert of Egypt in June 1985. His work completed, he found that his military flight home to his wife and baby daughter in Illinois had been canceled. Thus, he boarded the ill-fated flight 847 to Athens, planning to continue on to the States. Hijackers nearly destroyed those plans before he was able to escape. Kurt tells of his vision of Jesus during the intense pain from the beatings he suffered at their hands.

---

I had always been the typical Christmas-and-Easter-and-occasionally-with-the-folks churchgoer. I was a Christian, true enough, just not a very devout Christian.

Not anymore.

I had been kicked and beaten for an hour and a half. A .45 automatic was cocked at my head. I discovered what God is all about.

The hijacker kept saying, "One American must die." He meant me and had given me ten minutes to live.

"Dear Lord," I prayed, "please watch over Cheri and baby Meredith, now and after I am gone. Please be in their hearts and give them love, strength and happiness. Help Cheri always to remember me, but to find another someday so that Meredith will have a father. I love them so much, dear Lord."

Images of Cheri and Meredith flashed through my mind as I prayed. In one mental picture we were all together, and in another they were waving goodbye to me. Again and again I could see Meredith's face as I sat holding her out by the pool. She looked a lot like her dad.

I prayed then for myself. "Dear Lord, I've felt You at my side and pray that You will come into my heart. Please forgive my sins and protect me from further suffering. Give me the strength, dear Lord, to fight until I die."

I heard the pilot saying we had five minutes before the deadline.

I closed my eyes and slowed my breathing. My body was numb, almost paralyzed. I felt that I was close to death from my injuries. I asked the Lord to take me so that I would suffer no more.

Then a vision came into my mind. I could see a figure standing atop a hill of solidified black lava. His robes were blue and white, His face shadowed by the brightness surrounding Him. His arms, draped in His robes, were extended as if to receive me. And then I blacked out. I don't know how long I was out. I had lost track of time.

When I came to, my thoughts had changed. *I'm not going to just let them pick me up and shoot me. I'm going to give it one last shot.* Never in my life had I given up and quit.

The Lord is my strength and my shield; my heart trusts in him, and I am helped. My heart leaps for joy and I will give thanks to him in song.    Psalm 28:7

# The Bread of Life
## *Sue McConnaughay*

Sue McConnaughay was a 26-year-old housewife from Oak Park, Illinois, when this vision occurred. She describes her life at the time like this: "My marriage was on the rocks, and I kept getting pregnant." But God is in the business of restoring marriages, and Butch and Sue have experienced this firsthand. It was before the birth of their third child, while under doctor's orders to rest each afternoon, that she experienced this vision.

I was having a problem in my life, which involved many smaller problems and circumstances. I had success with some areas but still never seemed to get on top of the situation. I was discouraged. After victory in one area concerning submission to my husband, for instance, I found myself sliding into the same thing again. I didn't know what the problem was.

One afternoon after I had prayed about this, I was dozing when the Lord spoke so clearly it woke me up! He said, "Be hungry for My Word." I felt literally as if I were floating, and then the Lord said, "I am the Bread of Life."

I saw Him standing in front of me holding a loaf of bread on a breadboard. He kept handing me one slice of bread after another, but the loaf never got smaller. I saw that He was the answer to my problems for He will never run out of solutions!

I was willing to do anything the Lord said, but I was expecting a drastic request on His part. Now, I'm spending more time in Scripture, and less time worrying about what I'm supposed to be doing.

---

I sought the Lord, and he answered me; he delivered me from all my fears. Those who look to him are radiant; their faces are never covered with shame. . . . Taste and see that the Lord is good; blessed is the man who takes refuge in him. Fear the Lord, you his saints, for those who fear him lack nothing.

Psalm 34:4–5, 8–9

# About Mistakes
## *Catherine Marshall*

Catherine Marshall was the bestselling author of many great books including *A Man Called Peter, To Live Again,*

*Beyond Our Selves* and *Christy*. She also edited several books of prayers and sermons of her late husband, Peter Marshall.

---

It was during a period when an awareness of my own mistakes and wrong turnings gave me a sense of isolation from God. As I sat in a living room chair pondering this, there came to me a deep interior experience. I did not fall asleep, so this was no dream. Nor was it an otherworldly "vision." It seemed real, as real as the fabric on the chair, or the Florida sunlight pouring through the windows, or the trilling of a mockingbird in a tree outside. Suddenly, I felt the presence of Jesus.

"We're going on a journey," He told me.

Soon we were in a long, long room, like a throne room. Crowds of people lined the walls on either side. As we walked the length of the room approaching One whom I knew to be God the Father, I spotted in the crowd those I love who have gone on before me: my father, Peter Marshall, my grandson Peter Christopher—now not a baby, but a small boy, blond and dear.

Then I looked down at myself; to my horror I was dressed in rags—torn, unwashed, filthy. When we stopped before the throne, I could not even look up. I had never felt so unworthy.

In the same instant Jesus spread wide the voluminous robe He was wearing, completely covering me with it. (Interestingly, this was no kingly robe, rather, the roughest homespun material. I understood that until all His children are brought to glory, He continues to wear the robe of His humanity.)

"Now," He told me, "My Father does not see you at all—only Me. Not your sins, but My righteousness. I cover for you."

---

I will greatly rejoice in the Lord, my soul shall be joyful in my God; for he hath clothed me with the garments of salvation, he hath covered me with the robe of righteousness, as a bridegroom decketh himself with ornaments, and as a bride adorneth herself with her jewels.     Isaiah 61:10, KJV

# Child of Jesus
## *Irma Foster*

This beautiful experience, which occurred in Chicago, stayed with Irma Foster throughout her whole life, helping her through many hardships.

---

I was two-and-a-half years old when, because of necessity, my older sister and I were taken to Europe to stay with my grandparents. When we returned to America three years later my parents seemed unfamiliar to me, almost strangers, and I was a very unhappy, confused little girl. I had trouble adjusting and was often punished for, what seemed to me, even the slightest mistakes.

One day, after a very trying morning when I was six years old, my parents went out, taking my sister with them and leaving me home as punishment.

We lived on the second floor on a streetcar line next to the elevated train station on Chicago Avenue. I went to the front window, put my elbows on the sill and stared down on the street where people were rushing back and forth. I was very sad and finally I put my head down on my arms and cried until it seemed that my heart would break. I felt that no one loved me.

After I felt better I raised my head and looked up to the sky. I was astonished to see a shining figure, just the head and shoulders of One whom I later came to know as Jesus. The figure shone brightly and I was scared and fearful, but as I looked at the eyes I became conscious of love pouring out to me, such love as I had never experienced before, and a wonderful warmth enfolded me. I was filled with the ecstasy of joy. I looked down to the street and wondered why none of them saw what I did. His eyes also looked down to them and I was conscious of a message: "These, too, are My children."

From that time on, whenever things went wrong, I went to my room to be alone to think about my experience. And I always felt the wonderful warmth and love enfold me, reassure me and help me to understand, forgive and try harder to be good.

---

At that time the disciples came to Jesus and asked, "Who is the greatest in the kingdom of heaven?" He called a little child and had him stand among them. And he said: "I tell you the truth, unless you change and become like little children, you will never enter the kingdom of heaven. Therefore, whoever humbles himself like this child is the greatest in the kingdom of heaven. And whoever welcomes a little child like this in my name welcomes me."     Matthew 18:1–5

## Section 6

# In Answer to Prayer

# The Lord Appears to Solomon

This vision occurred after Solomon had finished building the Temple and his own palace. The Lord appeared to him at night and gave him this directive.

---

"I have heard your prayer and have chosen this place for myself as a temple for sacrifices.

"When I shut up the heavens so that there is no rain, or command locusts to devour the land or send a plague among my people, if my people, who are called by my name, will humble themselves and pray and seek my face and turn from their wicked ways, then will I hear from heaven and will forgive their sin and will heal their land. Now my eyes will be open and my ears attentive to the prayers offered in this place. I have chosen and consecrated this temple so that my Name may be there forever. My eyes and my heart will always be there.

"As for you, if you walk before me as David your father did, and do all I command, and observe my decrees and laws, I will establish your royal throne, as I covenanted with David your father when I said, 'You shall never fail to have a man to rule over Israel.'

"But if you turn away and forsake the decrees and commands I have given you and go off to serve other gods and worship them, then I will uproot Israel from my land, which I have given them, and will reject this temple I have consecrated for my Name."                    2 Chronicles 7:12–20

# Out of Africa
## *Clara Lewis*

Clara Lewis served as a missionary in Sinoe, Liberia, six degrees above the equator, for more than forty years. She continued in missionary service until her death at age 94.

James, one of the natives, married his deceased brother's wife (according to heathen custom) but was concerned because she was not a Christian. Mary was many years older than James and often ridiculed her husband because of his faith in the Lord Jesus Christ. She was an artist at nagging and made life miserable for her husband.

One day Mary became very ill and James came to the mission and asked us to pray. The entire church prayed for Mary's salvation in the evening service. The Lord answered and Mary was saved and healed.

Mary had a wonderful vision of heaven and we were

really surprised when she tried to explain what heaven was like. She had never attended the services or heard anyone preach the Gospel.

We asked her if they had lamps or lanterns in heaven. She replied, "No, they did not need lamps because the whole place was full of light. Jesus was there and His presence lit up the whole place. The Light shone past the sun, the stars and the moon. His clothes were white and shining. We always thought your clothes were pretty and white but now your clothes seem almost dirty."

This heavenly vision proved a great help to Mary and she loved and served the Lord Jesus Christ and was a blessing to many. She often longed and prayed to join the heavenly host and praise the Lord as they did in heaven.

---

There will be no more night. They will not need the light of a lamp or the light of the sun, for the Lord God will give them light. And they will reign for ever and ever.           Revelation 22:5

# The Two Looks
## *The Rev. Julius H. Massey*

Julius Massey spent his early career practicing law. After a "born again" experience, he began his religious studies.

He became pastor of St. Paul's Community Church in Plainfield, Illinois, where he served until his death in 1978.

---

I saw Jesus face to face.

Several times I had asked the Lord to give me a vision of Christ. One night I was awakened by someone gently tapping on the side of my mattress. I awakened instantly and saw Jesus just turning to walk along the side of the bed, to go to the foot. He was clothed with a dazzling white garment. His hair was auburn and came down to His shoulders.

His face was the most beautiful face I have ever seen, and on that face were two diametrically opposite looks. The one, the kind, compassionate look of the Savior, and the other the stern, majestic look of the King.

I was speechless. After about ten seconds Jesus "extinguished" Himself, that is, He went out like a light. I then said to myself that Jesus is the Savior of some and the judge of others. I understood more fully the Scripture that says the wicked will pray for rocks to fall on them to hide them from the face of Him who sits on the throne.

---

Then the kings of the earth, the princes, the generals, the rich, the mighty, and every slave and every free man hid in caves and among the rocks of the mountains. They called to the mountains and the rocks, "Fall on us and hide us from the face of him who sits on the throne and from the wrath of the Lamb! For the great day of their wrath has come, and who can stand?"                                    Revelation 6:15–17

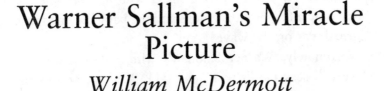

# Warner Sallman's Miracle Picture

## *William McDermott*

The late Warner Sallman, a Chicago artist, painted nearly two dozen oil paintings of scenes in Christ's life, the most famous being the "Head of Christ." He is also known for his wall-sized murals of Bible scenes.

Worried about an early morning deadline, Warner Sallman slept fitfully. Then he dreamed—a dream that taking form, shape and color became world-renowned.

Sallman's paintings of Christ decorate igloos of Eskimos and huts of the Hottentots. They can be found in cathedrals of different faiths in many lands. Sallman's mail often brought him testimonies from India, Africa, South America, Scandinavian countries, Canada, Australia and many other lands.

The story of this picture as well as of the artist himself is a miraculous one.

Back in 1917 a young commercial artist and a physician faced one another in the latter's office.

"The diagnosis is tuberculosis of the lymph glands. Surgery is your only hope," said the doctor. "Without surgery I believe you have about three months to live."

The artist left the office in a daze. His thoughts were not on himself but on the young singer who had become his bride only a few months before and the baby they had just learned was on the way.

Fortunately, Warner Sallman's wife was a Christian. "We will seek God's will," she said, "and we will thank Him for the three months. We will ask Him to use us to the limit and if He mercifully gives us more, we shall be grateful for it." Together and in complete calmness of spirit they went to their God in prayer.

Without surgery, God performed a miracle of healing. Even when he passed the age of seventy, Sallman's rugged figure and robust enthusiasm were often seen in churches where he delighted to do chalk illustrations of Christ.

Equally miraculous as his healing by the Lord was Sallman's experience in conceiving and drawing the head of Christ for which he is famous the world over.

From time to time he aided his church publishing house by preparing artwork for Sunday school papers. One day he was given an assignment to prepare a cover for one of these publications. He attempted to come up with an idea as he sat before his drawing board but nothing quite jelled as the deadline drew closer.

Now the thought flashed through his mind that he might make a sketch of Jesus for the cover illustration, showing the manly, cheerful, hope-inspiring Son of God and at the same time the humble, loving Savior.

By now only 24 hours remained before the drawing was due. Up in his attic studio that evening, he went to work and completed the first sketch. But it wasn't what he wanted. He did another and another. More followed as Sallman's nerves grew taut, his mind feverish.

He agonized in prayer but with no immediate answer.

At midnight he surrendered to apparent failure and threw himself on his bed. Finally he fell into a heavy sleep.

Then the miracle happened.

"In the early hours of the morning before dawn there emerged, in one illuminous moment, a visual picturization of Jesus, so clear and definite. And it appeared to me that I was seated at the drawing board with the completed drawing before me," said Sallman about that vision.

So real was the picture that Sallman was soon wide awake.

Hastily he went upstairs to his studio and made a thumbnail sketch before the image disappeared from his mind's eye. The next day he made an enlarged charcoal drawing, which he completed in time to make the deadline.

The Sunday school paper cover captured some attention but was soon forgotten. But the idea of picturing a manly Christ persisted with Sallman. Largely for his own amusement he decided to make an oil painting of the sketch. When it was completed, he placed it over the piano at his home.

One day, two representatives of a church publishing house came to interview him about doing some work for them. When Sallman let them in the door, both stopped abruptly to look at the picture of the head of Christ.

"This is exactly what we have been searching for," they said. With Sallman's permission, Fred M. Bates and Anthony W. Kriebel began the publication and distribution of the "Head of Christ."

By now the U.S. was deeply involved in World War II. Quickly the "Head of Christ" became a symbol of hope for the men and women of the armed forces. More than six million copies were sent to units all over the world.

Even in far-flung battle areas miracles accompanied the painting. In one instance two Americans captured in a skirmish were being hurried back to Japanese lines for interrogation. Bayonets prodded the GIs in the back and they dared not turn their heads.

In an effort to buoy his faith, one of the Americans started to whistle a gospel tune softly. Suddenly he heard someone behind him whistling the same tune.

Turning his head slightly, he heard a voice whispering in broken English.

"You Christian? We Christian, too. We know song you whistle. You turn quick, grab our guns. We surrender. No want to fight you."

The scheme worked. The Americans were able to take their willing captors back through their own lines and into the hands of American forces. Here they made an amazing discovery: The Japanese belonged to a Christian mission in Tokyo, the American to a church in Boston that had sent a large picture of Sallman's "Head of Christ" to the mission. The two shook hands as if feeling a covenant of

brotherhood in Christ and a lasting friendship was formed.
A stream of never-ending miracles appears to follow
Sallman's "Head of Christ."

---

May my tongue sing of your word, for all your commands are righteous. May your hand be ready to help me, for I have chosen your precepts. I long for your salvation, O Lord, and your law is my delight. Let me live that I may praise you, and may your laws sustain me.                                   Psalm 119:172–175

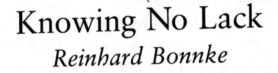

# Knowing No Lack
## *Reinhard Bonnke*

Reinhard Bonnke answered a mission call to Africa in 1967 at the age of 27. Since that time literally millions of Africans have made decisions for Christ and Reinhard has grown an almost unflappable confidence in God's willingness to provide for the work. The episode that follows describes part of the reason for his great enthusiasm. He had just borrowed money to purchase some furniture for needy pastors. The salesman skipped town, however, with the money. This was on his mind while driving and talking with the Lord one day. . . .

"If I had borrowed that money to enrich myself, I could understand why You allowed me to fall into that trap. But, Lord, You know that I borrowed it to help my brothers. I cannot understand why You allowed it."

Suddenly Jesus was tangibly in that old car. It was as if it became a flaming chariot filled with the glory and presence of God. I was no longer conscious of steering the vehicle, or of the passing scenery.

Then I heard a voice say, "The flour in the box shall not diminish and the oil in the cruse shall not become less."

Then the glory lifted. As I regained my composure those words began ringing in my heart. I knew what they meant.

"All right, Lord, my two mission accounts at the bank . . . one is the box and the other is the cruse. My duty is to pour them out. Your job is to fill them up."

(Note: God has honored his risk-all faith.)

---

"Praise be to the Lord, who has given rest to his people Israel just as he promised. Not one word has failed of all the good promises he gave through his servant Moses."                    1 Kings 8:56

*Section 7*

# Healing

# Saul Is Restored

Luke, also known as the beloved physician and author of the Gospel bearing his name, recorded this story in his book of The Acts of the Apostles.

---

In Damascus there was a disciple named Ananias. The Lord called to him in a vision, "Ananias!"

"Yes, Lord," he answered.

The Lord told him, "Go to the house of Judas on Straight Street and ask for a man from Tarsus named Saul, for he is praying. In a vision he has seen a man named Ananias come and place his hands on him to restore his sight."

"Lord," Ananias answered, "I have heard many reports about this man and all the harm he has done to your saints in Jerusalem. And he has come here with authority from the chief priests to arrest all who call on your name."

But the Lord said to Ananias, "Go! This man is my chosen instrument to carry my name before the Gentiles and their kings and before the people of Israel. I will show him how much he must suffer for my name."

Then Ananias went to the house and entered it. Placing his hands on Saul, he said, "Brother Saul, the Lord—Jesus, who appeared to you on the road as you were coming here—has sent me so that you may see again and be filled with the Holy Spirit." Immediately, something like scales fell from Saul's eyes, and he could see again. He got up and was baptized, and after taking some food, he regained his strength.

Acts 9:10–19

# Mrs. Boese Sees Again
## *The Chicago Tribune*

This newspaper account from May 1965 tells the story of Mary Boese. She had been blind for two years.

Mrs. Boese is a religious woman. She knew she would see again—even when doctors said she never would. Mrs. Boese said she had seen a vision of Christ and felt this was a sign her vision would be returned.

"He smiled at me.

"I knew because of the way He smiled at me that I would see again." She said she had the vision immediately after being examined by eye doctors in Oklahoma City. Three doctors had just told her she would never see again.

"I was totally blind at the time," she said. "My daughter was leading me down the hall. I saw this light coming toward me. It was a different kind. It glowed, and all at once there was Jesus standing there. He held His hands up in front of Him. He didn't say anything to me. I knew He didn't want me to come yet. I was ready."

. . . She happily recounted the moment her sight returned.

"I had gone into the bathroom about 5:40 A.M. I suddenly started to see things—toothpaste, a comb, towels around. There were so many things. I [assumed] that I had my glasses on and that my glasses certainly must have improved. I felt, and I didn't have any glasses on.

"I combed my hair for thirty minutes," she said. "It sounds vain, but two years is a long time not to see your hair."

---

He went to Nazareth, where he had been brought up, and on the Sabbath day he went into the synagogue, as was his custom. And he stood up to read. The scroll of the prophet Isaiah was handed to him. Unrolling it, he found the place where it is written: "The Spirit of the Lord is on me, because he has anointed me to preach good news to the poor. He has sent me to proclaim freedom for the prisoners and recovery of sight for the blind, to release the oppressed, to proclaim the year of the Lord's favor."    Luke 4:16–19

# The Healing Christ
## Genevieve Parkhurst

Genevieve Parkhurst, a clergyman's wife from Woodward, Oklahoma, had been told by her physician that she had a large lump in her right breast. Before she had set a date for surgery, Mrs. Parkhurst experienced the following. This story is told in her book, *The Healing Christ*.

One afternoon I stretched out on a bed, leaned against a pile of pillows and opened a new book. It was *You Are My Friends* by Frank Laubach. I do not remember what I read; it was something about the friendship of Jesus, but the pictures in the back of the book fascinated me.

Here were the great artists' conceptions of Jesus. There was "Christ Blessing the Children," by Plockhorst; "The Hope of the World," Copping; "Follow Me," the picture of the smiling Christ by Curry; "Christ at Thirty," by Hoffman; "The Son of Man," by Sallman. . . . With each, I grasped a fuller revelation of Jesus. He became so real that I was lost in His holiness and His love. I loved Him as I had never loved Him before, for I knew Him as I had not known Him before.

When I came to the picture of "Christ in the Garden," by Hoffman, the very heart went out of me. Jesus knew what I was facing. Oh, how He knew! He had faced death and said, "Not My will, but Thine be done." He had said, "No man taketh My life from Me. I lay it down of Myself." He had walked steadily to His cross. But He had died to redeem a world, while I was just going to die. Oh, that some good might come from my dying!

"O Christ, glorify Thyself through me," I prayed, pouring out my heart to Him.

Suddenly my breath stopped. I stared, spellbound, for there before me was the physical presence of Jesus. He was standing in a profile, His face lifted like the face in Hoffman's painting. I held my breath as that radiant face turned slowly, and His eyes looked straight into mine.

Oh! The eyes of Jesus! Nothing in this world can ever be as wonderful as His eyes. They held the wisdom of infinity, they were so understanding, so compassionate, so full of love. Those eyes held mine. They drank me, as the sun drinks the dew. I felt absorbed by His love. The room was full of light, and that light was His presence.

Illusion? Some might call it that. But what followed was no illusion. As I felt the oneness of being absorbed by Christ, there was a sharp stab of pain in my right breast. The fingers of pain ran down my side to my waist and out my arm to the elbow. My hand flew to my breast. My attention had turned to myself and when I again looked up the Presence was gone.

But the lump was gone, too! Completely gone! I laid

three fingers in the hole where the lump had been, pushing the loose skin into the emptiness.

Gone! There was no soreness, only an empty place. I took off my blouse and in amazement looked at the loose flesh that was left. I sat down trembling.

Why had such a thing happened to me? I was not worthy of such a blessing. I had not even prayed that He would heal me. It had not occurred to me. I believed that the Christian life was to give one strength to live and fortitude to die. This was an outpouring of pure grace, the evidence of divine favor, unasked for and unmerited.

I walked out and once more sought the mountaintop. But I walked on into life of His giving, from Gethsemane into Pentecost. So wonderful was the miracle that I could not speak of it. Jesus must have had a reason for telling those whom He healed to tell no one.

As the days passed, the tissues filled in according to the body's normal process of restoration. It took eight months for the process to be complete. Then it was perfect, and has been during the years that have passed.

---

Praise the Lord, O my soul; all my inmost being, praise his holy name. Praise the Lord, O my soul, and forget not all his benefits. He forgives all my sins and heals all my diseases; he redeems my life from the pit and crowns me with love and compassion.

Psalm 103:1–4

# The Shadow of Death
## *Carol Whisler*

Wycliffe missionary Carol Whisler tells of her dramatic encounter with a young Campa girl named Anita. The Campas are a tribal people numbering about 15,000. They live in the eastern foothills of the Andes in southern Peru.

---

I was working with other Wycliffe personnel in Peru with the goal of giving the Campas the New Testament in their language.

When I first saw Anita at the Peru Jungle Base in Yarinacocha, she looked twice her sixteen years. Suffering from nephritis, a kidney disease, and other ailments and weighing only 86 pounds, she was emaciated and vacant-eyed.

One Sunday afternoon in July while I was caring for her, she sat stiffly in a rocking chair by her bed stitching a dress. Suddenly, she seemed to lose her senses and her frail body shook in panic. "I'm going to die!" she shouted and began wailing wildly as her people do when death approaches. "My mother is eating the wastes of wild pigs!" she cried irrationally. This, I learned, brings an evil omen.

With trembling hands, I put her into bed and called the doctor. Hovering between life and death and delirious for several days, she suffered also from an inward struggle between the forces of Satan and her newfound faith. "I see Him. Now I don't see Him. The devil deceived me," she yelled. As her strength ebbed, her cries became fainter. "Jesus is good . . . no . . . no," she repeated over and over. Meanwhile, fellow workers at the jungle base joined me in prayer for her.

Friday dawned, gray and hopeless. But when I entered the room at four in the afternoon quiet prevailed. Anita's upturned face glowed and her arms stretched out toward a presence that those of us in the room could not see.

Hours passed. At midnight, she aroused us. "I'm hungry," she said. Like a starved child, she devoured the cereal drink I gave her. Gradually, she regained her strength.

How was it that she had new vigor, inner peace? "Anita," I asked her one day as we were reading the Campa Scripture, "did you see Jesus when you were so ill?" Her face lit up like a candle. "Yes, I saw Him. He said to me, 'My daughter, don't be afraid. I am with you.' There were many people with Him."

Having walked through the valley of the shadow of death with the Savior beside her, she now feared no evil. Christ had not only set her free, He had also made her whole.

------

The reason the Son of God appeared was to destroy the devil's work.                                    1 John 3:8

# The Day of Trouble
## *Charles Stilwell*

Pastor Charles Stilwell's spiritual biography is written with warmth, tenderness and great anticipation of the best in life through complete surrender to the plan of God. Charles reminds us that in the day of trouble, God hears our inward cry and supplies our every need.

---

During the summer between my first and second years of teaching, I tripped in a hole in the dark as I was taking care of the calves one night. The result was evidently a culmination of old injuries playing football and falling when in the cavalry troop.

After several visits to chiropractors to no avail, I went to an osteopathic physician and surgeon. He gave me several treatments, but on Sunday morning as we were getting ready for Sunday school and church, I fell in terrible pain. Bobbie quickly called the doctor and he arranged to see me immediately. After examination he said he was afraid he had done me more harm than good, for he thought that I had a ruptured disc and should get to an orthopedic surgeon immediately.

We arrived at the hospital and I went for tests. The

doctor explained to my wife and me that this would be a very serious operation. I would have to be in the hospital for two or three weeks. I would never be able to run or to lift anything again.

In the face of the unbelievable pain I was having, there was no doubt in our minds but that I should go ahead and have the surgery. It was scheduled for six o'clock the next morning.

Bobbie came to the hospital to see me before surgery. The doctor asked me how I felt and I said, "Fine. I have confidence in you and trust the Lord." He remarked that an attitude like that was very helpful to surgery.

When I came out from the anesthesia everything was beautiful to me. My wife was more beautiful than I had ever realized. The nurses were beautiful. Everything was good to look at and I was praising God. Then I saw Jesus on the ceiling of the room. His eyes were so loving and kind that I was infused with His love!

I had always been a quiet fellow, only said what was necessary to be said. I wasted no words. But now I was telling people of my love and appreciation for them.

On the third day after surgery my wife and the children came to see me as was their custom in the afternoon. She couldn't find me. I was not in my room, not even in my building. After some searching she finally found me in another building. I had walked there and I was witnessing to the men in that ward of the love and power of Jesus Christ! I who had always been reticent to witness for my Lord! I was telling them of His love. Bobbie, I think, was more amazed than I, and Chuck, to this day, tells people, "Dad was always quiet until after that operation. Now he tells everyone about Jesus."

We were learning that when God doesn't receive our full cooperation to heal in one way, He can still heal in another. Through my own choice I had undergone surgery, but it was God's healing in my body, mind and soul that was making me whole.

---

Some men brought to him a paralytic, lying on a mat. When Jesus saw their faith, he said to the paralytic, "Take heart, son; your sins are forgiven." At this, some of the teachers of the law said to themselves, "This fellow is blaspheming!" Knowing their thoughts, Jesus said, "Why do you entertain evil thoughts in your hearts? Which is easier: to say, 'Your sins are forgiven,' or to say, 'Get up and walk'? But so that you may know that the Son of Man has authority on earth to forgive sins. . . ." Then he said to the paralytic, "Get up, take your mat and go home." And the man got up and went home.     Matthew 9:2–7

# He Wants to Heal You
## *Dick Penner*

Dick Penner had suffered years of illness and had spent much time in a psychiatric ward. His daughters gave him and his wife, Elsie, a book called *I Believe in Miracles* by Kathryn Kuhlman. They talked Elsie into reading one of the stories, but her reaction was, "God doesn't heal anymore today because we have the Bible. He doesn't need to do that anymore." Then Dick and Elsie decided to attend a Kathryn Kuhlman meeting and he relates the following story.

---

I had never stood in line before. If I couldn't buy my way in, it wasn't worth going. But that day I took my pills, smoked my cigarettes and stood in line.

The doors opened and five thousand people flooded into the church. I had never cried in my life, but for some strange reason Elsie and I started weeping as soon as we got inside. We didn't understand it because we were tough people . . . a determined husband and wife who were making it even though they couldn't stand each other.

The organ played "Hallelujah" all morning long. I have no idea what Kathryn talked about, but halfway through the service an usher came and knelt down beside me. She whispered that God had revealed exactly what was wrong with me. She said that my vertebrae were deteriorating, my liver was sick and my lungs were black as tar. But then she said, "God is healing you."

I said, "I didn't come for that. I came for a little peace of mind because the doctors have given up on me and I'm going to die."

The lady assured me, "Jesus throws peace of mind in, but you are here and He wants to heal you."

Instantly I felt a hot, burning sensation in the back of my neck. Seeing my reaction she said, "What's wrong?"

I told her, "I think the fellow behind me just threw a cigarette at me."

She said, "No, Jesus is healing you. Stand up and do something you haven't done for years."

I threw my head back as hard as I could and there was no pain. The usher got excited and said, "Do something else you haven't done for a long time."

Well, I'd had bursitis so badly that I hadn't raised my right arm above my shoulder in two years. The arm went flying up.

Then the usher asked my wife, "Can I borrow him for a minute?"

Elsie answered, "You can have him." Elsie hadn't gotten saved yet.

Meanwhile, a medical doctor was on hand who validated all the miracles at the meeting. You had to go through him in order to get on stage with Kathryn Kuhlman.

I told him how I was an out-patient of a psychiatric ward, having suffered complete mental and physical breakdown. I showed him all the pills I was taking and he said, "That's authentic. You can take him up to see Kathryn."

Standing beside her I said, "Kathryn, how come I feel so light in here?" (I was referring to my chest area.)

She said, "Because Jesus has saved you. He has taken all the sins and thrown them in the sea of forgetfulness."

Then she reached over and said, "God bless you real good."

Suddenly I was on the floor.

When Kathryn gave an altar call, Elsie was the first one up to ask Jesus into her life. Later I asked her why.

She replied, "Because all through my Sunday school teaching career I've tried to teach people about the Holy Spirit. This morning I saw Him in the form of Jesus walking up and down the aisles touching people and healing them. I could hardly wait to meet Him in person and ask Him into my heart."

We checked out of the hotel and went to the car. But when I got behind the wheel something happened that was just as miraculous as what had occurred that morning. I reached over and took Elsie's hand. At that moment our marriage was healed. We have been on a honeymoon ever since November 23, 1973.

---

"For God so loved the world that he gave his one and only Son, that whoever believes in him shall not perish but have eternal life."　　　　　John 3:16

# The Divine Touch
## *Mark Buntain*
### *with Ron Hembree and Doug Brendel*

Mark Buntain was a respected American missionary who established major medical and educational institutions in India during 35 years of service there.

Nita Edwards, a lovely young Sri Lankan girl, was totally paralyzed from a tragic accident. Yet as she lay in bed hour after hour, month after month, the spirit of sadness gave way and she was given a beautiful channel of communication with her Lord.

---

Nita lay in her misery for four hours, wide awake, unable to escape into sleep. The soft sounds of the afternoon around her apartment filtered lightly into her room.

Suddenly at about four o'clock she heard a voice behind her. It was the most powerful tone she had ever heard. "Nita, I'm going to raise you up to make you a witness to Asia."

She was startled. If she had been able to, she would have jumped. She had thought she was alone in the room. Where had that voice come from? It said further: "I'm going to heal you on Friday the eleventh of February."

Nita's heart pounded. She was sure no one was in the room. She had never heard that voice before and felt an uncanny twinge in her spirit.

She struggled for the call button and buzzed for her attendant. If there was a man in the room, she wanted to know. . . . Perhaps under her bed? Nita made the girl get down on her hands and knees and look. No one was there.

Skeptically, but with excitement mounting slowly inside of her, Nita mentally checked off the possibilities. It could have been a dream, but she was wide awake. It could have been a hallucination, but she was not taking medication. It could have been her own imagination, but she wasn't in a good enough frame of mind to think up such a thing. The radio was off and there was no recording equipment around.

Which left two possible sources: God or the devil.

Nita had never taken kindly to people who proclaimed that God had spoken to them. She had always been suspicious of that whole realm of thinking. But deep in her heart, she already knew she had heard from God, that He was going to heal her on Friday, February 11, and that He had answered her prayers in a completely unique and thoroughly dramatic way.

Still, she just had to be sure.

So she prayed a hard-nosed, practical prayer: "Lord, I've heard this voice. If it's Yours, I want a confirmation."

She felt suddenly awkward, being so bold with the almighty Creator who had just promised to heal her and done so in an audible voice. But she thought of Gideon laying out his fleece and decided to press on with it.

"I want to hear the promise again," she prayed bravely. "In public. Let other people hear it, too."

She never mentioned the incident to anyone; never hinted that she had heard from God or that she was seeking a confirmation. But she steadily kept her heart open, worshiping her Lord for hours on end, day after day. . . .

[One Sunday Nita's brother, Colton, took her to church in a wheelchair.] He arranged for them to arrive early, so Nita could be situated in the choir loft between the piano and the wall—neither Colton nor Nita wanted her to be a spectacle. From her cubicle and with her vision problems, she could see very little of what went on, but in the divine plan she was really only there to hear one thing.

[It came as a prophetic message, spoken by one of the parishioners.] He lifted his voice and declared, "God will raise you up to be a witness to all of Asia. His word to you is true. Trust Him. He will not lead you astray. He will glorify Himself through you."

Nita's heart began to leap with joy. It was true. She had heard from God, and He had confirmed it—here, before fourteen hundred people. The very words that God had said to her.

Nita was ecstatic. Long after the crowd had cleared she was hoisted out of her little hole. And in her heart, she felt that there would be icing on the cake as well: He would speak to her further.

It was in this victorious frame of mind that Nita decided to ask for more information. As the nurse changed her bed linen the next morning, Nita was placed in her wheelchair. She sat by the window with the sunlight streaming in on the pages of her Bible and thought about the day she would be healed.

"Father, You told me the day and the date," she said simply. "Please, don't keep me waiting all day. Please tell me the time too."

She half-expected to hear the voice again, but heard nothing. Instead, a silent inner voice spoke to her spirit: She would be healed at 3:30 in the afternoon.

Nita thought she would burst with excitement. She had the date and the hour now—February 11 at 3:30 P.M. She was going to be healed by the power of God, and she was going to watch it happen.

How she would ever take the Gospel to Asia she had no idea. But of her healing, of the date and the hour, she was utterly sure. God had given her the supernatural gift of faith. In her mind the healing had already happened. All that remained was the gathering of the evidence!

In the past the afternoon sponging had always led to the same thing: The attendant would dress her in clean bed-clothes. But on February 11 Nita had a different idea.

"Bring me my slacks," she said.

As Nita slipped ever nearer to the heart of God, the chosen few she had asked to witness the miracle began to assemble around her.

At two o'clock, Colton and Suzanne arrived, solemn and quiet. They knew this would soon be holy ground. It was clear from the glow on Nita's face that the transformation would soon begin. They didn't talk to her at all, but sat down and began to pray quietly. . . .

Two women doctors stepped into the room. They were medical professionals who loved the Lord and who had examined and treated Nita during parts of her long ordeal. They had no hint of what was going to happen here; Colton had only invited them to a special time of prayer. They were honored. They knew Nita Edwards was in seclusion and only a select few had ever been behind these doors. . . .

The room was filled with prayer and a sense of awe, and the supernatural transformation began. The power of God invaded the room, from the right side of her bed, like a ball of fire. The glory of God burst in, flooding that tiny space with such intensity that the inhabitants were swept up in it and overcome by it. It was like looking directly at the noonday sun and only being able to take in a tiny fraction of the radiance.

The air was charged with a fantastic burst of electricity.

Nita felt what seemed like a million volts of power coursing through her body. Every cell, every fiber, every tissue pulsed with it. Wave after wave rolled through her. She was oblivious to her surroundings, to the others. She was longing to see Jesus.

Just at 3:30, He came into the room with blinding glory. Nita gazed into His face, and everything within her struggled to reach out to Him. Her healing was no more a factor. She was unaware of her physical condition. She longed only to touch Him . . . to connect somehow with that fabulous source of light and love.

As she looked at Him, He moved toward her. She was

suspended in time and space, filled beyond capacity by the unfathomable love of God. He came to the foot of her bed, and then He reached out with a nail-scarred hand and touched her. One time.

The chains of paralysis exploded away and Nita rocketed out over the end of her bed.

She landed on her knees with a thud, and her first sensation was the cold, hard tile floor beneath her. The divine warmth of the touch of her Lord had suddenly given way to this startling awakening. In the days to come she would realize that God had touched her so warmly only to thrust her into a ministry of fervent intercessory prayer in the cold real world.

Her knees had not been bent in over a year; now they were bent before Jesus. Her hands, useless for so long, were now straightened, raised up, worshiping God. Her voice had been still; now her mouth began to fill with heavenly words, tumbling out in a bubbly fountain of praise. For the first time in her life, she was leading others in prayer.

---

Yet he did not waver through unbelief regarding the promise of God, but was strengthened in his faith and gave glory to God, being fully persuaded that God had power to do what he had promised.

Romans 4:20–21

*Section 8*

# Entering the Kingdom

# The Transfiguration

Matthew, one of the Twelve, relates this event in his Gospel.

---

After six days Jesus took with him Peter, James and John the brother of James, and led them up a high mountain by themselves. There he was transfigured before them. His face shone like the sun, and his clothes became as white as the light. Just then there appeared before them Moses and Elijah, talking with Jesus.

Peter said to Jesus, "Lord, it is good for us to be here. If you wish, I will put up three shelters—one for you, one for Moses and one for Elijah."

While he was still speaking, a bright cloud enveloped them, and a voice from the cloud said, "This is my Son, whom I love; with him I am well pleased. Listen to him!"

When the disciples heard this, they fell facedown to the ground, terrified. But Jesus came and touched them. "Get up," he said. "Don't be afraid." When they looked up, they saw no one except Jesus.                Matthew 17:1–8

# The Night I Saw Jesus
## Zola Levitt

Zola Levitt is a musician, teacher, journalist and psychologist. This is taken from his book *Corned Beef, Knishes, and Christ* and occurred while he was wrestling with whether or not Jesus is truly the Messiah.

Jesus is a much taller man than I would have imagined. When I saw Him, He was wearing a maroon-colored robe, very ceremonious, hanging in folds like fine drapes. It stood open about six inches down the center, showing an off-white tunic underneath.

I was slumped down in an armchair where I had been reading and meditating. He was standing directly in front of me, and I had to crook my neck to look at His face. I remember thinking that He must have been very tall—6 feet 4 inches perhaps—because it was hard to look up so high. Alternately, I remember thinking that I must be seeing something unreal because the figure seemed entirely too tall for a man.

I was unable to make out His facial features at all. Either they disappeared into the ceiling or I was too shocked to see details. I did seem to be able to see His hair, which was light brown and waved gently down to His shoulders, rather like the great paintings of the Lord.

But I seemed somehow to perceive His expression: It was benevolent and good-humored. If He had spoken, He might have said, "Relax, I'm here, child."

But He didn't speak, and He didn't have to; I got the message.

Then, just at the instant I began to realize that I was looking Jesus Christ in the face, He disappeared. Vanished.

And I panicked because I went blind! I remember being relieved that the seeming apparition had disappeared, but I was looking into solid gray murk before my eyes. I couldn't focus on anything. It was like looking into clouds out of a plane. There was just nothing to be seen. I turned my head and looked at another angle but I still couldn't see.

Then everything came back with a pop. There was a sound, and my familiar bedroom came back to me.

My heart wasn't pounding and I didn't really feel too out of sorts, despite the eerie happening. I just sat there realizing I'd seen God. I was a little afraid to move.

I got my thoughts back together after a minute or so and I sort of tried to evaluate the event. "After all," I reasoned, "I've been sitting here reading a long time. I'm tired. Maybe I just drifted off to sleep for a moment. Maybe it was a dream. Maybe I just psyched myself up with my Bible reading and thinking about Christ. Maybe it was a kind of wishful daydream."

I had been deeply considering turning my life over to Christ. People had been witnessing to me, making me "see" the Lord. Perhaps in my skepticism I had conjured Him up in order to evaluate Him firsthand.

But I didn't really believe all that. I thought I'd really seen Christ. You can evaluate it as you like, but to me it was very real.

I can't remember if it was that same night that I finally went to Christ in prayer. I spent many nights in my bedroom armchair, reading the Bible and thinking about God and my life. You may think it was extraordinary that I could actually see Christ and still resist giving my life over to Him, but that's the stubbornness of my Jewish character. Thousands of my brothers in Israel resisted Him every day when He was there. (And thousands received Him, too, it should be remembered.) In more belligerent moments I used to tell smug Gentiles, "If it weren't for the courageous Jews who walked with Christ and formed your first churches, you wouldn't have any Christianity." (Probably they would have by some other of God's means. But my patience with Christians who curse the Jews is awfully thin.)

It was tough for me to come to Christ, and not because I was Jewish. It was mostly because I believed that I knew better how to run my affairs than He did. I fall back into that belief every other day, as things are now, even though I know it's ridiculous. For me, giving up on Zola Levitt and letting Jesus take over is the hard part. I gather we all have some trouble there.

The manner in which I finally "joined the flock" is a long story and I'll save it for later. I think it would serve better if I say something about the "old man," the one who died when Christ took over with His gift of rebirth, before getting to my big moment.

That "old man" is dead but he rolls in his grave. I often want to tell him to "Rest in Peace," because he never had any.

---

After this, Jesus went out and saw a tax collector by the name of Levi sitting at his tax booth. "Follow me," Jesus said to him, and Levi got up, left everything and followed him.          Luke 5:27–28

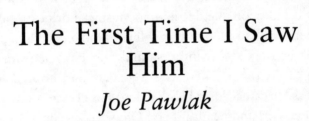

# The First Time I Saw Him

## *Joe Pawlak*

Joe Pawlak was a layman employed as an engineer in a Chicago plant. After the experience on Lake Michigan described here he left the industry and devoted his time to an evangelistic and healing ministry. Many people were healed by the Lord at his services. He went to be with the Lord in 1991.

---

I had a meeting with Jesus Christ in May 1969.

It was a beautiful, warm, sunny day. I realize now that

it was God who led me to go down to the lakefront to eat my lunch that afternoon. Many others were sitting on the benches eating their lunches as well. Fishermen were coming in displaying the huge fish they had caught.

I was about to pour my coffee and have a bite to eat when I looked out across Lake Michigan. All things began to disappear except for a direct line onto the lake and there was Jesus walking on the water toward me. He actually seemed taller than a telephone pole.

In the vision was a dimension of beautiful color that one is not able to see with the normal eye. He was wearing sandals, a beautiful red robe and a blue cape. His hair was dark auburn to His shoulders and His eyes were of the most beautiful color that I have ever seen. It was a blue that is indescribable. He had no mustache or beard, just a tiny line of hair along the jaw line; it looked as though an artist had taken a paintbrush and drawn a line from one side to the other. There was a golden aura around Jesus and as He came closer I looked into His eyes and saw love, compassion and beauty there. Oh, such loveliness!

He walked through the pier, the cars and people and stood at the hood of my car, holding His arms up as if He were praying over me and then He made the sign of the cross.

Then He looked to the left and disappeared.

Right then the old sinner in me died and I was born again. I did not understand all of this at the time because I had been raised a Roman Catholic and had not read the Bible. I didn't know that Jesus was appearing to people and that they were seeing visions. I didn't know that people could receive the gifts of the Spirit. I didn't know that people could be healed by Jesus.

For three days and nights I wept for joy.

---

He will stand and shepherd his flock in the strength of the Lord, in the majesty of the name of the Lord his God. And they will live securely, for then his greatness will reach to the ends of the earth. And he will be their peace. Micah 5:4–5

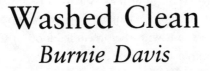

# Washed Clean
## *Burnie Davis*

Burnie Davis began his ministry at the age of eighteen. Soon he was praying for the sick, oftentimes in crowds of ten thousand. He tells here of an experience in Matamoros, Mexico, where he was conducting a crusade.

---

One night a woman came running to the altar when I presented the invitation for salvation. After she had repeated the sinner's prayer, she fell backward and lay quietly on the floor. Though her lips were moving, no audible words came forth. I felt impressed that she was having a vision.

After the service I talked with her about the experience

through the interpreter. She said that she had seen Jesus walking toward her with His hands cupped. When Jesus drew nearer to her, she saw that His hands were filled with blood and she knew that it was His own blood. Then she said that Jesus reached down to the inside of her and washed her with His own blood.

"And now I feel so clean," she said. Her face shone like the face of an angel. This was my first experience preaching on the mission field. We saw a great many outstanding miracles during that crusade.

---

> For you know that it was not with perishable things such as silver or gold that you were redeemed from the empty way of life handed down to you from your forefathers, but with the precious blood of Christ, a lamb without blemish or defect.     1 Peter 1:18–19

# Acceptance
## *Richard H. Rice*

Richard H. Rice, a member of St. Paul's Methodist Church in Kensington, Maryland, and an officer in the Fort Meade-Laurel chapter of the Full Gospel Business Men's

Fellowship International, served as an assistant secretary for a consulting engineer firm in Bethesda, Maryland.

------

The glory and grace of God began in my life when I was born July 26, 1945, with cerebral palsy. It has continued through the years, during which I have been steadily healed of the brain damage I suffered at birth. This healing is now complete beyond my wildest hopes.

I was in school when I realized that I was in serious trouble and headed straight for disaster if something were not done, and done quickly. This "something" came during study hall one evening in the form of a poem I read. The words got through to me and showed me that what I sought could be found only in Jesus Christ.

That summer I worked at a Christian camp for underprivileged children from the Washington, D.C., area. On my twenty-first birthday I went out for a celebration with another counselor after everyone had gone to bed. We returned around 11:30 just as a storm was beginning to brew. At midnight, a streak of lightning brightened the entire sky and above the cross on a nearby mountain there appeared to us a vision of Christ frowning.

I interpreted this to mean that I should turn around and accept the disciplined way of the Lord or face ultimate disaster. At the same time God assured me that if I stopped warring against Him, salvation would be mine. One week later, however, not having yet followed through as I should have, I awoke in the middle of the night with an anxiety attack. This really frightened me, and prepared my heart for the Lord Jesus to come in and start the cleansing process.

This event took place November 18, 1967, following a Sunday evening service in a Baptist church in New Hampshire. The spiritual "ice" melted, my heart became soft and I invited Jesus Christ into my life as my personal Lord and Savior.

Instantly I felt a great weight lifted from my shoulders and realized I was being freed from the hatred that had so long ruled my life. I felt peace and a wave of joy flowing like an ocean through my entire body. One month later Jesus revealed to me that I no longer needed cigarettes for a companion or to calm my nerves, and within three days I went from one-and-a-half packs a day to none.

> "Enter through the narrow gate. For wide is the gate and broad is the road that leads to destruction, and many enter through it. But small is the gate and narrow the road that leads to life, and only a few find it."
> Matthew 7:13–14

# The Calling
## *The Rev. Fred Steinmann*

Fred Steinmann was a preacher and well-known evangelist from Lockport, Illinois.

When I was a boy I lived with my parents on a farm near Joliet, Illinois, and spent a lot of time working with my dad. One day he told me he was going to the cornfield to husk corn and that he wanted me to stay and work at the barn.

Several hours later my dad came running, weeping. He said, "Come to the house with me, son. I want to tell you something that happened in the cornfield."

Then he told me the following: "While I was in the cornfield a great bright light came down around me and I became so fearful that I fell down on my face and tried to cover my eyes, but it was impossible. The light was as bright and penetrating under the clods of soil as it was above them. I looked up to call on God and there stood Jesus. I said to Him, 'I cannot look upon Your face because I am a sinful man.' I repented of all my sins right there and then Jesus touched me. I said to Him, 'I cannot speak good English, but I have a boy. I will give him to You and he can preach for You.' I felt that this was pleasing to the Lord."

God showed my father right then that someday I would be preaching the Gospel.

Later in life, after my conversion, I was lonely, sad and heavyhearted. It seemed that the closer I got to God the more trouble I had. My sister took care of me those times.

One day while working in the field I sat down to rest and read the Bible. I read, "Out of heaven he made thee to hear his voice, that he might instruct thee: and upon earth he showed thee his great fire; and thou heardest his words out of the midst of the fire" (Deuteronomy 4:36, KJV). God was speaking to Moses. I believed that God was speaking to me as well and that He would teach me and tell me things from heaven. I sincerely believed this, but I didn't know how it would be done.

Some months later in the early spring I was up in the hayloft praying, as this was a habit of mine. This day as I was talking to Jesus I told Him that I would not come up into the hayloft anymore, but that I still loved Him and would read my Bible. Then I began to pitch hay and as I pushed my fork into the stack of hay, I looked up and saw a large beautiful rose appear above it. The petals began to open up and as they opened tongues of fire shot from them to the top of the barn. I was afraid the barn would catch on fire as it was full of hay and alfalfa.

What a horrible sight watching the flames shooting into the air! Then out of the rose and flames came the figure of a man. I realized it was Jesus. As He looked at me He moved slowly toward me and said, "Go preach the Gospel and I will be with you."

His eyes caught my eyes and I said, "Yes, Lord, I will go." After that the vision lifted and Jesus disappeared.

A few years later, during the Depression, I was preaching in the slums of 30th and State Streets in Chicago. Many days I would be without food and sometimes had to sleep in hallways. One day I was in the Chicago Loop, hungry and with only five cents in my pocket. I saw a little restaurant that posted a menu offering a five-cent bowl of soup.

I went in and a waitress came up to me, looking at me as though I were some sort of strange creature. She asked what I would have and I told her just a bowl of soup. She asked what I wanted for the rest of my meal. I repeated, "Just the soup."

In a few minutes she brought the soup and platters of food. Without a word she placed a feast before me and I said only a word of thanks to the Lord. As I started to eat, Jesus appeared across the table from me, just as plain as He had in the rose in the barnyard. He raised His hands as if in blessing, then vanished. After I had finished eating, I called the waitress over and told her I had no money to pay for all the food.

"Who asked you for any money?" she snapped.

I was curious and asked her why she had brought all that food and why she had looked at me so strangely when I came in.

"Well, that's the funny thing," she said. "As you walked into this place, someone said to me, 'Feed that man. Give him all he can eat, whether he can pay for it or not.' And I did."

"Do you know who it was who spoke to you?"

"No," she said, somewhat sharply.

"It was Jesus," I told her. "I saw Him while I ate. If you don't know Him you should, because He died for you. I don't know a thing about you, miss, but I know you're a sinner. Whatever sins you have, Jesus died to forgive."

Tears began to come down her face and I asked her not to cry because of the people in the restaurant. Before I left, I asked her to accept the Lord into her life and told her that if she did, I would surely see her in heaven. As

I left, she was still standing there, wiping her eyes with her apron.

———

Yet when I preach the gospel, I cannot boast, for I am compelled to preach. Woe to me if I do not preach the gospel! 1 Corinthians 9:16

*Section 9*

# Worshiping Jesus

# John's Heavenly Vision

This scene of worship in heaven was given to the apostle John while he was in exile on the Island of Patmos during the last years of his life.

---

Then I looked and heard the voice of many angels, numbering thousands upon thousands, and ten thousand times ten thousand. They encircled the throne and the living creatures and the elders. In a loud voice they sang: "Worthy is the Lamb, who was slain, to receive power and wealth and wisdom and strength and honor and glory and praise!"

Then I heard every creature in heaven and on earth and under the earth and on the sea, and all that is in them, singing: "To him who sits on the throne and to the Lamb be praise and honor and glory and power, for ever and ever!" The four living creatures said, "Amen," and the elders fell down and worshiped.     Revelation 5:11–14

# True Worship
## *The Rev. Roxanne Brant*

Prior to her preparation for the ministry, Roxanne Brant was studying to be a concert pianist and medical doctor. One day while studying in a library, however, she had a powerful confrontation with Christ that changed her from a militant agnostic into a Christian. In addition to her studies at Gordon Divinity School, she studied at Harvard Divinity School and Boston University School of Theology.

---

Several years ago something very supernatural and unforgettable occurred that left a mark on me. It taught me that my first ministry is to the Lord and that to praise Him without worshiping Him is not enough. The Lord Himself came and showed me these things; He taught me the difference between praise and worship.

It happened one evening while I was ministering in a Presbyterian church. The songleader had led the congregation for about twenty minutes in the usual songs of praise and thanksgiving to God for healing, prospering and saving people—songs such as "Amazing Grace," "He Touched Me," "Blessed Assurance" and others.

When it was time to speak, the minister arose and began

to introduce me. Suddenly, to the right of the minister I saw Jesus. He was standing there with the loneliest expression I have ever seen on any face. His soft brown eyes overflowed with tears, which began to pour down His cheeks and drop silently at His feet. There was no noise, no sobbing and no movement except the tears as they silently streamed down His face and dropped to the floor. The sense of His loneliness filled my being and I wanted to comfort Him. How lonely He was, even in the midst of all His people!

He disappeared as suddenly as He had appeared, but I knew in an instant why He had been weeping. He was lonely because in spite of all our singing about Him, He Himself was completely ignored. No wonder He wept; of course He was lonely. My mind was so filled with what I had seen that when I came to the realization that I had just been introduced to the congregation, I seemed unable to speak. I arose and turned to the people, still choking down the sobs that filled me, but I managed to speak several words. All I could say was, "Now, let's worship Jesus."

Immediately it seemed as if the Holy Spirit flooded the sanctuary and began to move like a soft wind through a giant, divine harp. For the next fifteen to twenty minutes everyone in the congregation began singing as the Holy Spirit led them—such exquisitely beautiful arrangements as no human mind could conceive. The Holy Spirit was using us as instruments for the expression of His own worship to the Lord Jesus Christ. He had heard our feeble attempts to praise Jesus, but now He filled our vocal apparatus with His own perfect, holy songs of worship.

How indispensable we were to each other, the Spirit and each of us! I remember, particularly, how a man on one side of the auditorium and a woman on the other kept singing cascades of prophetic worship up and down the scale in perfect harmony as they worshiped the Lord. It sounded as if passages out of the book of Revelation were being brought to life. There was such a glorious, festal presence of the Holy Spirit that we felt as if we were in a heavenly banquet and that any minute we could put our hand on the arm of the King of kings and march right up the aisle with Him.

After some time, the Holy Spirit gradually lifted His hand from us and I knew that it was time for the message. Again, Jesus spoke very clearly to me and said, "You have ministered to Me, so now I will minister to you." Then I arose and gave a message on "Ministering to the Lord."

I share this because I am convinced that Jesus is all too frequently lonely at the services we claim to hold in His name. So many services are centered only in praise, which generally speaks of what God has done for us, but can ignore His presence with us. This is not enough, for we also need services that are centered in worship, a worship in which the believer is caught up in the present reality of God's Person, in the reality of who He is.

---

Jesus declared, . . . "Yet a time is coming and has now come when the true worshipers will worship the Father in spirit and truth, for they are the kind of worshipers the Father seeks. God is spirit, and his worshipers must worship in spirit and in truth."

John 4:21, 23–24

# Hallelujah!
## *Vaughn Besnyl*

After many years in Ethiopia, Vaughn, an Armenian, came to America. He tells the following story.

After a period of financial difficulty in my life, I began to feel my inadequacy in dealing with my problems. Something was missing from my life. I often had dreams with special meanings, and in January 1970 I dreamed that a friend of forty years came to me and kissed me on my forehead.

As I discussed this with my wife the next morning she asked me his name.

"Hampartsoum," I replied.

Carolyn is not Armenian. "What does that mean?" she asked.

"Resurrection or rebirth."

Later, going to my store, I prayed with earnestness and dedicated my life to the Lord. I knew that He had given me new birth.

One day a man entered my store and said, "I was putting gas in my car and something urged me to come in here. Are you a Christian?"

I told him that I was and for three months he came back again and again to talk with me and to offer an invitation. "Be my guest at a Full Gospel Business Men's dinner at our Covina chapter. If you do, I'll never bother you again." Finally I accepted his offer.

The meeting was strange—all those people with their hands in the air looking at the ceiling. I looked up and said to myself, *They see something that I don't.*

I couldn't sleep all that night.

The next month I went to another FGBMFI dinner meeting. The crowd was singing "Hallelujah." I closed my eyes and raised my hands along with everyone else. Suddenly I saw a vision of Jesus all dressed in white. He placed His left hand on my head and baptized me in His Holy Spirit.

I gasped aloud, "He's alive! He's alive!" My life has not been the same since.

At eight o'clock the next morning I went to my store. When I opened my desk drawer I saw a painting of Jesus that was exactly as I had seen Him in my vision. Startled, I thought God must have put it there.

Later I learned that my pastor had given it to one of my salesmen for me. I have a copy of that picture in my home, in my office and in my car.

I used to make promises to God in times of trouble and then forget Him. Not anymore: Not only His picture, but Jesus Himself goes with me everywhere I go. He lives in me.

Not long after Jesus appeared to me, Carolyn received a phone call urging her to rush to the hospital. Our son, Randy, had been injured seriously while riding a skateboard. He suffered a concussion, broken ribs, an injured knee and possibly a broken pelvis.

The next morning before going to the hospital I went to the store to pray. I told the Lord, "I've accepted You. You are my Lord. Please heal my boy. Show me Your power. I'm going to the hospital to see You heal our son."

When I entered his hospital room Randy was asleep. I awakened him and found him confused as to why he was in the hospital. He had no pain and was feeling fine.

The doctor came in. He couldn't believe what he found. Although X rays taken the preceding day had shown Randy's broken ribs and the concussion, now nothing was wrong.

The doctor turned to him and asked, "What is your name?"

"Randy."

He continued testing. "How much is five and five?"

"Ten."

"One hundred times two?"

"Two hundred."

The doctor turned to me and exclaimed, "This must be God, Vaughn! You must have been praying for him. You can take him home."

---

"I have come to bring fire on the earth, and how I wish it were already kindled! But I have a baptism to undergo, and how distressed I am until it is completed!"                                    Luke 12:49–50

# He Touched Me
## *Thomas May*

Thomas May was saved in 1973 and miraculously delivered from drugs and alcohol. He has served as an associate and youth pastor in an Assemblies of God church in his native Chicago and now works with campus ministries.

---

In early 1981, while enrolled in North Central Bible College, I attended some meetings at what was then known as the Minneapolis Gospel Tabernacle.

One speaker was a missionary to India named Mark Buntain. I found a seat in the front and listened as he preached vigorously on the healing power of Jesus Christ. He gave several remarkable accounts of people being completely healed of terminal cancer and other fatal diseases. It seemed that after each testimony we felt a new level of faith. These testimonies were life-giving! Praise and worship began to explode through the crowd.

As we rejoiced I heard these words: *You don't believe this.* I ignored the voice and continued to worship. Again

I heard, *You don't believe this.* Soon I realized it was the Holy Spirit speaking to me.

"Yes, I do, Lord!" I said, but He rebuked me and said that in reality I did not believe. Convicted, I could clearly see now, because of the atmosphere of great faith in the meeting, that I did not have faith beyond those walls, in the outside world. My faith in the actual healing of cancer was particularly weak.

I asked Him, "Lord, why don't I believe completely?" He then began to reveal to me that I was stuck in unbelief because I had hardened my heart over my father's death of cancer some years before. I learned that I was resentful toward the Lord for taking my father.

I offered this hurt and sin to the Lord immediately. I was quickly forgiven and was being restored when the Holy Spirit reminded me of one of my Bible college friends, Tom, who was fighting lymphoid cancer and was in the meeting. I recognized that the Holy Spirit was leading me to intercessory prayer that instant! I was given a tremendous burden to pray for Tom and believe for his healing. The Lord said to me, *He is healed.*

I was seated in the aisle seat and from the time that the Holy Spirit first started to speak to me I had not opened my eyes. All of a sudden it was as if I could see behind me and I could see Jesus standing at the entrance of the sanctuary. At that very second the missionary, still preaching, said, "Jesus is in the room right now!"

"Yes, He is!" I said. I saw Jesus walking down the aisle touching all those who reached out to Him with their faith.

Again the missionary spoke. "He is passing out gifts for

all those who will receive!" I saw Jesus walk by me to the front and over to the other aisle. I knew He had touched me.

We continued to worship at an intense level. Next thing I knew I heard a thud. I opened my eyes and there was my friend, Tom, the cancer patient, lying on the floor not far from me knocked off his feet by the power of the presence of Jesus. His eyes were closed and his lips seemed to be moving in prayer. Knowing Tom wasn't the zealous or emotional type, it was clear that the Lord was doing a work in him. Then the Lord said to me, *Go tell him that he is healed.*

I asked God to use the speaker to tell Tom instead of me. The Lord said, *No, you do it!*

I asked the Lord to call on the pastor and then the associate pastor, but each time His response was the same: *No, you do it!*

I confessed, "Lord, I can't do it!"

The Holy Spirit replied, *That's right, you can't do it, but I can. So testify of what you have witnessed.*

Then I knew that, because I had witnessed His presence, I could indeed tell my friend with full confidence that he was healed. I did and we rejoiced together in agreement with the reviving presence of the Holy Spirit.

---

" 'If you can'?" said Jesus. "Everything is possible for him who believes." Immediately the boy's father exclaimed, "I do believe; help me overcome my unbelief!"                    Mark 9:23–24

*Section 10*

# Called to Serve

# The Lord Calls Samuel

Samuel's birth was an answer to his mother's prayers. In thanks to the Lord, Hannah dedicated the child to His service as she had promised. From the time he was weaned he lived in the Temple and grew to become a great prophet and judge of the people of Israel.

---

The boy Samuel ministered before the Lord under Eli. In those days the word of the Lord was rare; there were not many visions.

One night Eli, whose eyes were becoming so weak that he could barely see, was lying down in his usual place. The lamp of God had not yet gone out, and Samuel was lying down in the temple of the Lord, where the ark of God was. Then the Lord called Samuel.

Samuel answered, "Here I am." And he ran to Eli and said, "Here I am; you called me."

But Eli said, "I did not call; go back and lie down." So he went and lay down.

Again the Lord called, "Samuel!" And Samuel got up and went to Eli and said, "Here I am; you called me."

"My son," Eli said, "I did not call; go back and lie down."

Now Samuel did not yet know the Lord: The word of the Lord had not yet been revealed to him.

The Lord called Samuel a third time, and Samuel got up and went to Eli and said, "Here I am; you called me."

Then Eli realized that the Lord was calling the boy. So Eli told Samuel, "Go and lie down, and if he calls you, say, 'Speak, Lord, for your servant is listening.' " So Samuel went and lay down in his place.

The Lord came and stood there, calling as at the other times, "Samuel! Samuel!"

Then Samuel said, "Speak, for your servant is listening."

And the Lord said to Samuel: "See, I am about to do something in Israel that will make the ears of everyone who hears of it tingle. . . ."                    1 Samuel 3:1–11

# The Stairway
## *The Rev. Norris Wogen*

The Reverend Norris Wogen was the organizer and president of the first and second International Lutheran Conferences on the Holy Spirit held in Minneapolis, Minnesota. He has traveled and lectured extensively in this country and in Europe.

When I was of confirmation age, between twelve and fourteen years of age, I had my initial call to go into the ministry. This is rather common. In the old Evangelical Lutheran Church a survey was conducted some years back and they discovered that about sixty percent of the ELC ministers had received their initial call of God for the ministry at confirmation age. One of my brothers who is also a pastor received his initial call to the ministry at about the same age.

It was then that I had a vision of Jesus. He was standing at the top of a huge golden stairway that reached into the heavens. He was standing there in His glory with a long robe. On either side of this stairway was an honor guard of angels flying up and down, giving the impression of a living ribbon. There was no sound, just the indescribable beauty of glory and majesty. My relationship to God during this time was so great that I used to pray that God would not let me be successful in anything else—that He would force me into the ministry if necessary.

I never shared this vision with anyone until about two years ago. I was the twelfth child in a family of thirteen and knew from other experiences that I would be laughed at and this was too precious to me to be ridiculed by anyone. This vision has been a source of inspiration for me down through the years.

---

[Jacob] had a dream in which he saw a stairway resting on the earth, with its top reaching to heaven, and the angels of God were ascending and descending on it. There above it stood the Lord, and he said: "I am the Lord, the God of your father Abraham and the God of Isaac. I will give you and your descendants the land on which you are lying." Genesis 28:12–13

# The Shaping of an Apostle
## The Rev. June Newman Davis

The visions that June Davis describes here and in her book, *The Shaping of an Apostle,* encouraged her through many unhappy events in her life. After her salvation, she felt an overwhelming desire to be obedient in service to God.

Every time I began to pray, since giving my heart to Jesus, His presence engulfed me with a love—a belonging that I had never known.

Four days after my conversion, while lying on my bed praying in the dark, I began to see (before my eyes) a vision in glowing, vivid colors. Over my bed I saw the folded "nailprint" hands. Then my eyes followed up in a circular path as more of Jesus came gradually into view. First His right arm and shoulder appeared, then His glorious, beautiful, glowing face. I noticed even the pink in His cheeks. The other shoulder and arm appeared next and then my eyes focused on His hands again.

I don't know how long the visible presence of the Lord in vibrant colors was over my bed. I do know that I studied His face. He had the most beautiful eyes I had ever seen: They were blue, like deep pools of water. This surprised me. I had thought He would have brown eyes. His brown hair, parted in the center, was filled with golden highlights and fell softly in a few waves to His shoulders. He had a mustache, which was sparse, and His beard was not too full; it looked as though some was missing in the center as it parted on His chin.

Over His shoulders was a purplish-blue robe with red highlights, under which was a white undergarment showing at the neckline. He was seated, with His hands folded. I was told later that "sitting" means a work is finished. I felt that as a vessel I had been broken and it was time for the remolding process to begin.

As I beheld the Lord with my natural eyes I began to cry with joy and exclaimed, "Oh, Jesus, You are so beautiful! I thought You were supposed to be ugly and not to be desired." He smiled. All the time I was speaking to Him, I thought I was lying prone in the air over my bed. It was a glorious time, and one that I will never forget.

One week after my first vision of Jesus, He appeared to me again in the daytime while I was sitting at my kitchen table reading the Bible. I looked up and saw Him standing on the other side of the room. He had on His white servant's attire with a rope tied around His waist. This time He appeared in a sepia color.

He walked up to me and began to speak in an audible voice, "June, study and make yourself approved unto Me" (2 Timothy 2:15). I jumped up from my chair, shaking violently. I could see right through Him and yet He was there. His voice was clear.

Trembling I asked, "How do I know this is real?" If I had not been pinned in between the table and chairs I would probably have fallen flat on my face.

He answered me, "You must have faith-*faith-faith!*" With these words, He pounded His fist into the palm of His other hand and the most tremendous feeling went through me, stronger and stronger each time He said the word *faith*. I believe He zapped me with the gift of faith at that moment, because I had faith to believe Him for anything for myself and others from then on. He knew there would still be more of Midian—a desert experience—for me to go through.

During this time I had many unhappy things going on in my natural life. When I prayed, however, Jesus took away my pain and heartache and lifted me up into the heavenlies. Often my children would come in and find me crying with joy. They could not understand it.

It was during one of those distressing times when I poured out my heart to the Savior that I felt Someone's hand on me. I turned and there was Jesus sitting on the side of my bed beside me dressed in white. Such a phenomenal peace flowed through me. I can't remember if it was during this visitation or before that He said to me, "I will keep him in perfect peace whose mind is stayed on Me" (Isaiah 26:3). This is how He taught me many Scriptures. Every one of them was branded into my memory with a supernatural experience. . . .

I began reading the Bible all the time. I asked a friend how I might have more understanding of what I was reading and she said, "Start quoting James 1:5 and John 14:26 every day before you begin. And ask the Lord to anoint your understanding to receive the truth He has for you that day."

It wasn't too long before I was seeing glorious results from that prayer. Things were beginning to come together and every Bible study I attended was a banquet feast to me.

There were many revelations at first—five visions of Jesus in the first six months of my walk with Him!

One of them was quite astounding to me because I had not yet read the book of Revelation.

At a convention one night Kevin Ranaghan was speaking under a powerful anointing on the Lordship of Jesus. All of a sudden, all three thousand people in that ballroom stood to their feet and began praising the Lord.

As I stood there doing the same—but with my eyes open because I had never seen or felt anything like this before—the whole ceiling disappeared. There on a cloud in a very blue sky stood the "Glorified Christ" (Revelation 1:13-15). He had white wool hair, glistening white garments, a golden girdle from His waist to His hips and fire shooting out of His eyes, straight at me!

It was magnificent. I thought everyone could see Him as I did; He was so plain to see. He stood there as if He was drinking in all the praise and receiving it unto Himself. His arms were down, His palms showing and His fingers close together.

At that moment I believed I was seeing God and I thought, *Well, now I am going to die because I have seen God.* I guess I thought that because He did not look as He had in the other visions with brown hair and blue eyes. . . .

Many have told me that they have seen Jesus standing alongside of me or standing over me as I minister to people. In New Zealand, for instance, as I spoke in a Presbyterian church, the first man I ministered to after speaking that evening said, "I have to tell you something. While you were speaking in the pulpit, Jesus was standing behind you all the time in a brilliant light." The Lord has often revealed Himself this way to those who need to know that even though I am a woman and a stranger, I am His servant.

---

"My food," said Jesus, "is to do the will of him who sent me and to finish his work. Do you not say, 'Four months more and then the harvest'? I tell you, open your eyes and look at the fields! They are ripe for harvest." John 4:34–35

# His Crown
## *Charles Stilwell*

Charles Stilwell and his wife, Bobbie, founded the Home Ministry Fellowship, Inc., in Pearce, Arizona.

---

One evening as I meditated at sunset in the church, Jesus appeared before me in a vision. His eyes seemed to see clear through me. They were transparent, and I became transparent before Him. I sat for some time just drinking in His love and His beauty. Then He spoke to me.

"Charles," He said, "see what you are doing to My crown."

I hadn't even noticed that He had a crown. Now I saw the crown of thorns unraveling and falling gracefully around His shoulders. There was a sadness in His voice as He continued.

"Charles, I really did die for you." Slowly the crown of thorns again entwined itself and lay upon His head in perfect order. Then He disappeared.

As I sat in the quietness of that church I realized that I had ceased to emphasize His death upon the cross for me and for my people. I had fallen prey to the simple definition of the atonement as "at-one-ment." It sounded pretty, but there was no redemption in it. He was willing to suffer and die and shed His blood for me and for every one of my flock.

As I sat there meditating on this vision I realized that He had taken all my sins, all my sorrows, all my sufferings, all my diseases upon Himself when He was nailed to that cross. By His blood He had redeemed me, had paid a ransom for me, had bought me back from the enemy, Satan. He did that all for me. That was the atonement. It isn't possible to be "at-one" with Him unless we accept His forgiveness and His salvation through His blood.

A bloodless religion brings no redemption. I had taken away His salvation when I failed to acknowledge that He really *did* die for me.

That began to change my ministry. I began to preach salvation, encompassing healing for the body and mind as well as for the soul.

---

For what I received I passed on to you as of first importance: that Christ died for our sins according to the Scriptures, that he was buried, that he was raised on the third day according to the Scriptures.

1 Corinthians 15:3–4

# Afterword

If these testimonies have pointed out to you the reality of the living and loving Lord and Savior Jesus Christ, and you wish to receive Him as your personal Lord and Savior, pray the following prayer:

Almighty and most merciful God, I thank You for sending Your Son, Jesus Christ, who died for my sins and arose again from the dead that I might live eternally with Him. I am truly sorry for everything that I have done wrong and I ask You to forgive me, and I forgive everyone who has wronged me. I now ask You to make me a Christian. I open my heart to You and ask You to come in and live forever with me. I want to live for You and ask You to guide me in all Your ways from this day forward. As I read Your Word, may Your Holy Spirit teach me and draw me closer in love to You and to my fellow man to the glory of Your holy name. Thank You, Jesus. Amen.

If you prayed this prayer and would like some additional literature, please write us at Grace Lutheran Church, Attention: Pastor Nylander, 950 S. York Rd., Bensenville, IL 60106-3230.

# Copyright Acknowledgments

"The Sights of Paradise," copyright © 1978 by Richard E. Eby, D.O., is taken from *Caught Up into Paradise* and used by permission of Fleming H. Revell Company.

"In the Master's Presence," taken from *Within Heaven's Gates* by Rebecca Springer, copyright © 1984 by Whitaker House, is used with permission.

"The Doors of Heaven" is taken from *My Glimpse of Eternity*, copyright © 1977 by Betty Malz, and used by permission of Chosen Books.

"The Fields Are White Unto Harvest" is used by permission of Lillian Wiley.

"Heaven and the Angels" is taken from *Heaven and the Angels* by H. A. Baker and used by permission of Osterbus Publishing House.

"Blessed Aleyde" is taken from *These Women Walked with God*, by Fr. M. Raymond, copyright © 1956 by Benzinger, Bruce and Glencoe, Inc., and used with permission.

"Different Worlds" is reprinted from Full Gospel Business Men's *Voice*, September 1985 issue, and used with permission.

"The Rising of My Soul" is used by permission of the Christian Missionary Society.

"The Commission" is used by permission of the World Missionary Assistance Plan.

"His Open Arms," formerly titled "A Voice from the Military," is reprinted from Full Gospel Business Men's *Voice*, July-August 1970 issue, and used with permission.

"Between Two Wills" is used by permission of Kent W. Nylander.

"A Changed Life" is used by permission of Dorothy Adams.

"Taken by Surprise," from *The Journal of John Wesley*, is used by permission of Moody Press.

"The Question," copyright © 1975 by Monica Furlong, is used by permission of Coward, McCann & Geoghegan, Inc.

"The Glory of God," copyright © 1986 by Charles and Frances Hunter, is taken from *His Power Through You* and used by permission of Hunter Books.

"F. B. Meyer and the Keys to Life," copyright © 1956 by Dr. Benjamin T. Browne, is taken from *Let There Be Light* and used by permission of Fleming H. Revell Company.

"God's Plowman" is taken from "How $10 Was Multiplied into Millions" by Cathy Garlit and reprinted by permission of *The Pentecostal Evangel*.

"I Dreamed About Jesus" is used by permission of Norma Owak.

"The Hijacking," from *One American Must Die*, copyright © 1986 by Kurt Carlson, is reprinted by permission of Congdon & Weed, Inc.

"The Bread of Life" is used by permission of Sue McConnaughay.

"About Mistakes" by Catherine Marshall is reprinted with permission from *Guideposts* magazine. Copyright © 1972 by Guideposts Associates, Inc., Carmel, New York 10512.

"Child of Jesus" is used by permission of Irma Foster.

"Out of Africa" is used by permission of Clara Lewis.

"The Two Looks" is used by permission of Julius Massey.

"Warner Sallman's Miracle Picture," taken from "The Miracle Picture," is copyright © 1963 by *Christian Life* magazine and used by permission.

"Knowing No Lack" is reprinted from Full Gospel Business Men's *Voice,* July 1985 issue, and used by permission.

"Mrs. Boese Sees Again" is copyrighted © 1965 Chicago Tribune Company, all rights reserved, used with permission.

"The Healing Christ" is taken from *The Healing Christ* by Genevieve Parkhurst, copyright © 1964 by Macalester Park Publishing Co. and used with permission.

"The Shadow of Death" is taken from *Translation* magazine, copyright © 1971, and used by permission of Wycliffe Bible Translators, Inc.

"The Day of Trouble" is used by permission of Pastor C. Stilwell of the Home Ministry Fellowship, Inc.

"He Wants to Heal You" is reprinted from Full Gospel Business Men's *Voice* used by permission.

"The Divine Touch" is reprinted by permission from *Miracle in the Mirror* by Mark Buntain, published and copyrighted © 1982 by Bethany House Publishers, Minneapolis, Minnesota 55438.

"The Night I Saw Jesus," copyright © 1975 by Zola Levitt is used by permission of Tyndale House Publishers.

"The First Time I Saw Him" is used by permission of Joe Pawlak.

"Washed Clean" is taken from *How to Activate Miracles in Your Life and Ministry* by Burnie Davis, copyright © 1982 by Harrison House, Inc., and used with permission.

"Acceptance" is reprinted from Full Gospel Business Men's *Voice*, June 1974 issue, and is used with permission.

"The Calling" is used by permission of the Rev. Fred Steinmann.

"True Worship" is taken from *Ministering to the Lord* by Roxanne Brant, copyright © 1973 by Northern Florida Christian Center, Inc., and used with permission.

"Hallelujah!" is reprinted from Full Gospel Business Men's *Voice*, September 1985 issue, and used with permission.

"He Touched Me" is used by permission of Thomas May.

"The Stairway" is used by permission of the Rev. Norris Wogen.

"The Shaping of an Apostle" is used by permission of the Rev. June Newman Davis.

"His Crown" is used by permission of Charles Stilwell.